Gendered Vulnerabilities and Violence in Forced Migration

Mohammad Musfequs Salehin

Gendered Vulnerabilities and Violence in Forced Migration

The Rohingya from Myanmar

Mohammad Musfequs Salehin
Centre for Peace Studies
UiT The Arctic University of Norway
Tromsø, Norway

ISBN 978-3-031-62437-7   ISBN 978-3-031-62435-3 (eBook)
https://doi.org/10.1007/978-3-031-62435-3

© The Editor(s) (if applicable) and The Author(s) 2024. This book is an open access publication.

Open Access This book is licensed under the terms of the Creative Commons Attribution 4.0 International License (http://creativecommons.org/licenses/by/4.0/), which permits use, sharing, adaptation, distribution and reproduction in any medium or format, as long as you give appropriate credit to the original author(s) and the source, provide a link to the Creative Commons license and indicate if changes were made.

The images or other third party material in this book are included in the book's Creative Commons license, unless indicated otherwise in a credit line to the material. If material is not included in the book's Creative Commons license and your intended use is not permitted by statutory regulation or exceeds the permitted use, you will need to obtain permission directly from the copyright holder.

The use of general descriptive names, registered names, trademarks, service marks, etc. in this publication does not imply, even in the absence of a specific statement, that such names are exempt from the relevant protective laws and regulations and therefore free for general use.

The publisher, the authors and the editors are safe to assume that the advice and information in this book are believed to be true and accurate at the date of publication. Neither the publisher nor the authors or the editors give a warranty, expressed or implied, with respect to the material contained herein or for any errors or omissions that may have been made. The publisher remains neutral with regard to jurisdictional claims in published maps and institutional affiliations.

Cover illustration: Pattern © Melisa Hasan

This Palgrave Macmillan imprint is published by the registered company Springer Nature Switzerland AG.
The registered company address is: Gewerbestrasse 11, 6330 Cham, Switzerland

Paper in this product is recyclable.

This book is dedicated to the Rohingya people of Myanmar and their right to self-identity and citizenship.

Acknowledgements

Over the years, I have been privileged to receive support from numerous individuals and institutions, without whom the completion of this research and manuscript would not have been possible.

This research was conducted as part of a broader initiative on 'Stateless in Bengali Borderlands', at the Peace Research Institute Oslo (PRIO) and funded by the Norwegian Research Council, along with personal research grants from the Centre for Peace Studies (CPS), UiT the Arctic University of Norway. I am grateful for this financial support, which played a pivotal role in bringing this project to fruition.

Special gratitude is extended to the University Library of UiT the Arctic University of Norway, for their generous funding, enabling this book to be accessible as an open resource.

I owe a debt of gratitude to my esteemed colleagues Zerihun Woldeselassie, Kara Kathleen Hodgson, Arsalan Bilal, and the anonymous reviewer for their meticulous reading of the manuscript and valuable insights.

For their assistance during the crucial fieldwork stage in Cox's Bazar, I extend my sincere appreciation to Mohammad Bellal Hossain and Shah Alam Sakib at Dhaka University; Shakawat Hossain, Tasnuva Ahmad, and Azizul Hoque at Centre for Peace and Justice (CPJ), BRAC University; Ayesha Siddika at the Asian University of Women; and Aslam Hossain and Mizanur Rahman at UiT the Arctic University of Norway. Their invaluable contributions significantly helped with conducting the research.

The journey to publication was made smoother by the unwavering support of the editorial team at Palgrave, to whom I extend my heartfelt thanks.

Lastly, my deepest appreciation goes to my wife Samina and my two sons, Saihan and Nubaid, for their enduring patience and understanding during the challenging phases of research and manuscript preparation.

About the Book

The Rohingya, primarily a Muslim minority group from the Rakhine State in Myanmar, are one of the largest stateless people in the world, with nearly one million people alone living in neighbouring Bangladesh. This anthology explores the gender dimensions of violence and the vulnerabilities of the Rohingya, both in Myanmar and in Bangladesh. Along a continuum of violence, Rohingya men and women have experienced different forms of direct, structural, cultural, and symbolic violence at different times and in different spaces. While in Myanmar, both men and women experienced murder and physical injury. Men also faced torture and bondage labour, while women were additionally subjected to rape, harassment, and groping, mainly perpetrated by the Myanmar military. Through the othering process, both men and women became constructed as *Bengali Kala*. However, the threat constructed through this othering was gendered. Men were portrayed as rapists, extremists, and threats to Buddhist nationalism; women were constructed as ugly and fertile breeders; hence, their sexuality, reproduction, and motherhood had to be controlled by the military. Both men and women experienced gender-based movement restrictions, deprivation of education, and other services in Myanmar. When they reached Bangladesh as forced migrants, women continued to bear the scars of violence and faced different structural, symbolic, and cultural violence, that is, victims of multiple and child marriages, dowry, and domestic violence. Experiences of everyday security (safety, well-being) in the camps were also gendered. In their host communities, an

x ABOUT THE BOOK

othering process is also underway, connected mainly to rising criminality and violence in the camps, and economic and social pressure on the host community. In this process, Rohingya men have become constructed as 'a monstrous other', connected to insecurity, illicit drug traders, and possible Islamist militants, while women have become represented as vulnerable and victims of violence.

CONTENTS

1 **Introduction**   1
The Research   4
Organisation of the Book   5
References   8

2 **Gender, Violence, and Vulnerabilities in Forced Migration: A Multi-dimensional Approach**   11
Introduction   11
Gendered Vulnerabilities, Violence, and Migration   13
Sexual and Gender-Based Violence (SGBV)   14
Structural, Cultural, and Symbolic Violence   15
Structural Violence, Intersectionality and the Continuum of Violence   19
Conclusion   21
References   22

3 **The Rohingya Crisis: Background on Myanmar, the Current Conflict, and Relevant Actors**   27
Introduction   27
Background to the Rohingya Crisis   28
Actors in Conflict: The Ultranationalist Buddhists and ARSA   32
The State, the Military and the Monks: A Complex Interplay   36
Conclusion   38
References   39

xii CONTENTS

4 Gendered and Racialised Vulnerabilities and Violence Against the Rohingya in Myanmar — 45

Introduction — 46

'Monstrous Other', Rohingya Men, and the Existential Threat to Buddhism — 46

Bengali Kala: From Everyday Racism to Political Rhetoric in Myanmar — 49

Gendered Rumours, Rohingya Women, the Military, and the Ultra-Buddhist Nationalists — 51

Rohingya Women, Vulnerabilities, and Sexual Violence — 53

Sexual Violence Against Rohingya Men and Boys — 56

Gendered Mobility, Discrimination, and Justice — 58

Intermarriage, Women, and the Monks — 60

Buddhist Women in the Ultranationalist Movement — 61

Other Forms of Violence — 62

Conclusion — 63

References — 65

5 Gendered Vulnerabilities and Violence in Rohingya Refugee Camps in Bangladesh — 69

Introduction — 69

From Shaming and Ignorance to Domestic Violence — 70

Multiple Marriages, Child Marriages, and High Fertility — 73

From Personal Hygiene to Mental Trauma — 78

Access to Justice and Gender Issues in the Camps — 80

ARSA, Gangs, Insecurity, and Women Refugees — 82

Rohingya Men in Bangladesh: 'Monstrous Other' on the Creation — 85

Ordinary and Empowered Rohingya Women: Unpacking Complexities — 86

Conclusion — 88

References — 90

6 Conclusion — 93

References — 101

Index — 103

ABOUT THE AUTHOR

Mohammad Musfequs Salehin is an associate professor at the Centre for Peace Studies, UiT the Arctic University of Norway. Salehin also serves as a senior researcher at the Peace Research Institute Oslo (PRIO), where he leads a research project funded by the Norwegian Research Council (NFR) on 'Statelessness in Bengali Borderlands: New Technologies and Challenges for Identity and Identification'. He holds a PhD in Sociology from the University of Sydney, Australia. His research and teaching expertise encompasses migration, refugees, statelessness and new technologies, women and gender issues, development and non-state actors, memoryscapes, politics, and peace. Salehin was a visiting research fellow at the Refugee Studies Centre (RSC), University of Oxford, UK, during the Trinity term in 2023.

ABBREVIATIONS

APBn	Armed Police Battalion
ARSA	Arakan Rohingya Salvation Army
CiC	Camp-in-Charge
CPJ	Centre for Peace and Justice, BRAC University
GBV	Gender-based Violence
GoB	Government of Bangladesh
HRW	Human Rights Watch
ICC	International Criminal Court
ICG	International Crisis Group
IOM	International Organization for Migration
Ma Ba Tha	The Organization for the Protection of Race and Religion
NDPD	National Democratic Party for Development
RLO	Refugee-led organisation
RNDP	Rakhine Nationalities Development Party
RRRC	Refugee Relief and Repatriation Commissioner
RSO	The Rohingya Solidarity Organisation
SLORC	State Law and Order Restoration Council
TDH	Terre des hommes
UN	United Nations
UNHCR	United Nations High Commissioner for Refugees
USDP	Union Solidarity and Development Party

CHAPTER 1

Introduction

Abstract Gendered vulnerabilities and violence are intrinsically linked with forced migration. This chapter introduces the book's main aim, which is to examine the gendered dynamics of violence experienced by the Rohingya people, first during the conflict in the Rakhine State of Myanmar, then after their forced migration to Bangladesh. It provides a brief overview of the context and the imperative to investigate the gendered dimension of Rohingya forced migration, emphasising the nature and extent of gendered vulnerabilities and violence, both in the country of origin and in the country of destination, as a continuous process. Additionally, it delineates the methodology employed in the research conducted for this book.

Keywords Rohingya • Forced migration • Gender • Violence

Every year millions of people are forcefully displaced around the world and, in mid-2023, the number reached 110 million people (UNHCR, 2023). Various factors such as violence, conflict, war, religious or ethnic persecution, gross human rights violations, and environmental issues, including climate change, have contributed to this forced displacement or forced migration. In forced migration, individuals fall prey to various forms of violence across their country of origin, transit routes, and destination countries. The experience of violence[1]—whether direct (i.e., physical injury, psychological harm, sexual violence), structural (i.e., patriarchy,

© The Author(s) 2024   1
M. M. Salehin, *Gendered Vulnerabilities and Violence in Forced Migration*, https://doi.org/10.1007/978-3-031-62435-3_1

poverty, intimate partner violence), cultural (i.e., the underlying logic that justifies violence such as religion, ideology) (Galtung, 1969, 1990, 1996), or symbolic (i.e. masculine domination and its recognition as 'natural order') (Bourdieu, 1979; Bourdieu & Wacquant, 2004)—varies based on gender and other intersectional identities.

Gendered vulnerabilities and violence, such as instances of rape, sexual assault, human trafficking, slavery, harmful traditional practices, forced marriages, early and/or multiple marriages, and honour killings, are regrettably becoming more prevalent amid large-scale conflicts and warfare, which often lead to forced migration. For example, after the onset of conflict in Ukraine, women who were displaced experienced a significantly higher incidence of gender-based violence—nearly three times more than non-displaced residents (15.2 percent compared to 5.3 percent) (Capasso et al., 2022). In some earlier conflicts, sexual violence against women was used as a tactic of war. In Rwanda, an estimated 100,000 to 250,000 women experienced rape during the three months of the genocide. In Sierra Leone (1991–2002), the figure reached approximately 60,000 women, over 40,000 in Liberia (1989–2003), up to 60,000 in the former Yugoslavia (1992–1995), and a minimum of 200,000 in the Democratic Republic of the Congo since 1998 (United Nations, 2014). The effects of such violence are lasting and extend even after the end of the conflict. Psychological trauma, pregnancy resulting from rape, war children, sexually transmitted diseases, social stigma, fragmentation in social and familial ties, traumatic memories, and disruptions in livelihood are some of aftermath effects that most of the victims experience. Moreover, sexual and gender-based violence can continue, and even increase, after the conflict. This book uses a gender lens to explore the different forms of violence experienced by forced migrants such as Rohingya people, who were forcefully displaced from the Rakhine State of Myanmar to Bangladesh. In particular, it takes a closer look to explain how and why violence against the Rohingya is gendered.

The Rohingya, a primarily Muslim[2] minority from the Rakhine State[3] of Myanmar, are the world's largest stateless people. For nearly 50 years, the population in Rakhine State—one of the seven states in Myanmar— struggled under repressive military rule and ethno-religious tensions between the Rakhine Buddhists and Rohingya Muslims. Many Buddhists in Rakhine State, as well as other parts of the country, have claimed to feel threatened by the Muslim population and have been intent on forcing the Rohingya and other Muslims out of Myanmar, which they consider their exclusive ancestral land (Fortify Rights, 2014). Ultra-Buddhist nationalist groups, such as the '969' movement and Ma Ba Tha (Organisation for the Protection of Race and Religion), primarily directed their religious chauvinism at Islam and Muslims. Their slogans, such as 'Burma for the Burmans' and 'To be Burman is to be Buddhist', as well as the depiction of Muslims as 'mad dogs', illustrate their advocacy for the protection of Buddhism from the perceived threat of Islam and the consequent expulsion of Rohingya from Myanmar (Office of the United Nations High Commissioner for Human Rights, 2019; UN IIMM, 2024).[4] These tensions have led to substantial outbreaks of violence and carefully orchestrated arson attacks in Rakhine State since 2012, directed at the Rohingya population and other Muslim communities (Fortify Rights, 2014). Human rights organisations estimate that inter-communal violence in mid-2012 displaced around 125,000 mainly Muslim people in Rakhine State (Human Rights Watch, 2013). Nevertheless, then-President Thein Sein in July 2012 suggested that the 'only solution' to the troubles in Rakhine State was either to send the stateless Rohingya to third countries or to contain them in UNHCR-administered camps (Brinham, 2012).

Due to the inability and unwillingness of the Myanmar authorities to address the ramifications of the 2012 violence, violence erupted again in 2013, 2016, and 2017. In Rakhine State, the Rohingya faced atrocities including murder, killings, rape, and other forms of sexual violence (Haar et al., 2019). These episodes led to the forced migration of about one million Rohingya refugees to neighbouring Bangladesh. In 2017 alone, about 700,000 Rohingya[5] refugees fled to Bangladesh, about half of whom (around 52 percent) were women and children; one in every six Rohingya refugee households is headed by a single mother. Although, traditionally, women have been considered more empowered in Myanmar than in other Southeast Asian countries, 'in reality, the place of women in Burmese society is more tenuous than many purport' (McKay & Win, 2018, p. 2). The intersections of race, ethnicity, religion, and gender raise important questions when analysing extremist nationalist ideologies (e.g., '969' and Ma Ba Tha) as part of a populist project that mobilises huge support from the ordinary Burmese Buddhists to construct Muslim Rohingya men, in particular, as a 'fearsome other' and to consequently legitimise violence against the Muslim Rohingya. Yet, the precarious Rohingya have continued to face vulnerabilities and violence in their country of 'safe destination', Bangladesh. Therefore, the Rohingya experienced a continuum of different forms of violence in different times and spaces. Several research projects[6] have already taken place to explain the causes and consequences of the Rohingya crisis. Nevertheless, the structural, cultural, and symbolic forms of violence and their gendered dimensions have relatively been unexplored. In addition, research on the continuum of gendered vulnerabilities and violence experienced by the Rohingya is also scarce. This book seeks to fill that gap by exploring the gendered experiences of violence and vulnerabilities by the Rohingya in their country of origin as well as in their host country as a 'continuum of violence' (Cockburn, 2004; Kelly, 1987; Kostovicova et al., 2020). In doing so, it employs Galtung's (Galtung, 1969, 1990, 1996) and Bourdieu's (Bourdieu, 1979) conceptualisations of violence to more fully understand the violence against the Rohingya. Therefore, this book aims to unpack the gendered dimensions of the crisis by focusing on the nature and extent of gendered vulnerabilities and violence in the context of Rohingya forced migration, both in their country of origin and in their country of destination, as a continuous process.

THE RESEARCH

The main aim of this book is to examine the gendered dynamics of the conflict in the Rakhine State of Myanmar and the consequent forced migration of the Rohingya to Bangladesh, with a particular focus on the different types of violence (direct, structural, cultural, and symbolic violence) experienced by the Rohingya along a continuum. Therefore, it also explores the gendered vulnerability and violence at the refugee camps in Bangladesh. When looking at the gender dimensions of the conflict and violence in the two different settings, this book attempts to understand what makes this conflict and the experiences of violence gendered and racialised. In what ways do the nationalist sentiments that are promoted speak to the efficacy of the gendered and racialised narratives in fostering conflict and violence in Rakhine? How and why are the experiences of violence in refugee camps in Cox's Bazar gendered?

To answer these questions, I conducted fieldwork in Rohingya refugee camps in Cox's Bazar three times over five years. I employed qualitative research techniques to understand the conflict from the bottom up, from the position of the people in their communities and their everyday experiences. This approach allowed for greater, and ideally culturally appropriate, access to everyday life. It also facilitated a clearer understanding of how conflict and peace processes and related institutions have affected individuals, communities, and society. For this research, I recruited participants through snowball sampling. A total of 55 individuals were interviewed. In December 2018, I conducted ethnographic fieldwork in both the Kutupalong Rohingya camps in Ukhia and Cox's Bazar in Bangladesh using semi-structured interviews, participant observation, focus group discussions and key informant interviews. I did additional interviews with the Rohingya refugees and local communities in Cox's Bazar in January 2022 and March 2023. I conducted several in-depth interviews with the women and men[7] in the Rohingya camps in Cox's Bazar. I also interviewed the Imam of the local mosque, *Majhi*, leaders of refugee-led organisations, and Rohingya female health workers. During my visits to the camps, I had several informal conversations with many inhabitants of the camps, as well as with local people in Ukhia and Cox's Bazar, regarding the crisis. To supplement the data collected through fieldwork, I used online newspapers (published in English), academic articles, books, and other secondary sources including published and unpublished government and non-governmental documents on Rohingya issues. A thematic analysis was applied to analyse the data.

Researching the Rohingya crisis was not an easy task on many grounds. Initially, it was difficult to get access to the camps, due mainly to the administrative restrictions from the government of Bangladesh. However, several gatekeepers, including individuals and institutions (e.g., the Centre for Peace and Justice at BRAC University) working with Rohingya issues, facilitated my access to the field. Other problems were centred around the nature of research that talks about violence, in general, and about the gendered dimensions of violence, in particular. In this regard, my female research assistant played a significant role in facilitating the access, discussion, and collection of data. Although difficult, I remained sensitive to ethical issues such as ensuring confidentiality and employing empathy while researching violence and gender (Morgan & Björkert, 2006). In this book, all the names of the respondents used are pseudonyms and all personal data were anonymised to ensure their confidentiality and safety.

ORGANISATION OF THE BOOK

This book is structured into six chapters, each contributing to a nuanced comprehension of the complex Rohingya crisis and the gender-specific vulnerabilities inherent within scenarios of forced migration and displacement.

Chapter 1 introduced the key aim of the study, the ethnic group under consideration—the Rohingya, and the topic of gendered violence. It then provided an overview of the research design of the study and presented the research questions that guided it.

In Chap. 2, a concise analysis of different conceptualisations of violence is presented, delineating the intricate web of gender-specific vulnerabilities entwined within forced migration and displacement. This section employs an intersectional and 'violence continuum' approach to examine the intricate nuances of gender dynamics and violence within the refugee landscape, drawing upon Bourdieu's and Johan Galtung's conceptual frameworks on violence.

Chapter 3 delves into the core of the Rohingya crisis, spotlighting the watershed event of the mass exodus of forcibly displaced Rohingya to Bangladesh in 2017. Beyond simply outlining the conflict and displacement, this chapter illuminates the historical underpinnings and the spectrum of key stakeholders involved. It describes the roles played by the state, the military, the ultra-nationalist Buddhists, and the Arakan Rohingya Salvation Army (ARSA), as well as the complex interplay among these entities in Myanmar.

Chapter 4 interrogates the underlying gender-specific ideologies that allow violence to perpetuate against the Rohingya. It navigates through the labyrinth of gendered rumours, ultra-nationalism, and military and Buddhist politics in Rakhine State, revealing the prevalence of sexual violence against the Rohingya community. This chapter also reflects on gendered mobility, discrimination, and justice, as well as how they are rooted in societal and institutional structures. It analyses the dynamics and politics of intermarriage, reproduction, and Rohingya motherhood. Finally, it unravels the construction of the Rohingya men as the 'Monstrous Other' who is perceived as an existential threat to Buddhism.

Chapter 5 focuses on the multidimensional gendered vulnerabilities that besiege the Rohingya populace within the refugee camps of Cox's Bazar. This segment scrutinises issues such as societal shaming, pervasive ignorance, psychological distress, and the endemic prevalence of domestic violence within the Rohingya community, illustrating how and why they are gendered. It expounds upon the prevalence and rationales behind multiple marriages and child marriages, alongside the multifaceted challenges pertaining to personal hygiene and psychological trauma. It then considers the issues of gendered mobility and justice in the camps in Cox's Bazar. Moreover, it investigates the gendered dimensions of the role of ARSA, the pervasive sense of insecurity, and the perpetuation within the host community of the narrative of Rohingya men as the 'Monstrous Other'.

The final chapter amalgamates the pivotal arguments elucidated in the book, shedding light on how gender-specific and intersectional identities unveil the vulnerabilities entrenched in the plight of the Rohingya people. It culminates by proposing potential sustainable solutions for this multi-faceted crisis.

NOTES

1. Here I used the famous Norwegian sociologist and one of the founding fathers of Peace Studies, John Galtung's, classification of violence namely direct, structural and cultural violence. A detailed discussion on Galtung's conceptualisation of violence is presented in Chap. 2. For a better understanding of his concepts, see, Galtung, J. (1969). Violence, Peace, and Peace Research. *Journal of Peace Research*, 6(3), 167–191. http://www.jstor.org/stable/422690, Galtung, J. (1990). Cultural Violence. *Journal of Peace Research*, 27(3), 291–305. https://doi.org/10.117 7/0022343390027003005, Galtung, J. (1996). *Peace by Peaceful Means: Peace and Conflict, Development and Civilization* https://doi.org/10.4135/9781446221631
2. The Rohingya people of Myanmar are primarily Muslim, but a small of number Rohingya are Hindu.
3. Rakhine is one of the eight major ethnic groups of Myanmar recognized by the government and constitutes the majority of Rakhine state population.
4. For a detailed discussion on the ultra-Buddhist nationalists and various actors in the Rohingya Crisis, see Chap. 3.
5. According to the Refugee Relief and Repatriation Commissioner (RRRC) of the Government of Bangladesh, there are now 967,842 registered Rohingya Refugees living in different camps in Ukhia and Teknaf of Cox's Bazar District of Bangladesh. About 52 percent of them are women. For latest statistics, see www.rrrc.gov.bd
6. See, for example, Jobair Alam, 'The current Rohingya crisis in Myanmar in historical perspective', *Journal of Muslim Minority Affairs*, 39:1, 2019 pp. 1–25; Nick Cheesman, 'How in Myanmar "national races" came to surpass citizenship and exclude Rohingya', *Journal of Contemporary Asia*, 47:3, 2017, pp. 461–483; Nehginpao Kipgen, 'Ethnicity in Myanmar and its importance to the success of democracy', *Ethnopolitics: Formerly Global Review of Ethnopolitics*, 14:1, 2015, pp. 19–31; Nehginpao Kipgen, 'Conflict in Rakhine State in Myanmar: Rohingya Muslims' conundrum', *Journal of Muslim Minority Affairs* 33: 2, 2013, pp. 298–310; Syeda Naushin Parnini, 'The crisis of the Rohingya as a Muslim minority in Myanmar and bilateral relations with Bangladesh', *Journal of Muslim Minority Affairs*, 33:2, 2013,

pp. 281–297; Md. Ali Siddiquee, 'The portrayal of the Rohingya genocide and refugee crisis in the age of post-truth politics', *Asian Journal of Comparative Politics*, 5: 2, June 2020, pp. 89–103; Ardeth Maung Thawnghmung, 'The politics of indigeneity in Myanmar: competing narratives in Rakhine state', *Asian Ethnicity*, 17:4, 2016 pp. 527–547;, AKM Ahsan Ullah, 'Rohingya refugees to Bangladesh: historical exclusions and contemporary marginalization', *Journal of Immigrant & Refugee Studies*, 9:2, 2011, pp. 139–161; Anthony Ware and Costas Laoutides, *Myanmar's 'Rohingya' conflict* (New York: Oxford University Press, 2018).

7. I acknowledge that there are some sexual minorities among the Rohingya. The most known sexual minority is transgender (*hijra*) people. However, it was not possible to reach the transgender (*hijra*) Rohingya during my research. Other sexual minorities are not either well-known or discussed topics among the Rohingya due mainly to their traditional and Islamic social structure.

REFERENCES

Bourdieu, P. (1979). Symbolic Power. *Critique of Anthropology, 4*(13–14), 77–85. https://doi.org/10.1177/0308275x7900401307

Bourdieu, P., & Wacquant, L. (2004). Symbolic Violence. In N. Scheper-Hughes & P. Bourgois (Eds.), *Violence in War and Peace: An Anthology* (pp. 271–274). Wiley-Blackwell.

Brinham, N. (2012). The Conveniently Forgotten Human Rights of the Rohingya. *Forced Migration Review, 41*, 40–41.

Capasso, A., Skipalska, H., Chakrabarti, U., Guttmacher, S., Navario, P., & Castillo, T. P. (2022). *Patterns of Gender-Based Violence in Conflict-Affected Ukraine: A Descriptive Analysis of Internally Displaced and Local Women Receiving Psychosocial Services* [NP21549-NP21572].

Cockburn, C. (2004). The Continuum of Violence: A Gender Perspective on War and Peace. In W. Giles (Ed.), *Sites of Violence: Gender and Conflict Zones* (pp. 24–44). University of California Press. https://doi.org/10.1525/california/9780520230729.003.0002

Fortify Rights. (2014). *Policies of Persecution: Ending Abusive State Policies Against Rohingya Muslims in Myanmar*, 79, www.fortifyrights.org

Galtung, J. (1969). Violence, Peace, and Peace Research. *Journal of Peace Research, 6*(3), 167–191. http://www.jstor.org/stable/422690

Galtung, J. (1990). Cultural Violence. *Journal of Peace Research, 27*(3), 291–305. https://doi.org/10.1177/0022343390027003005

Galtung, J. (1996). Peace by Peaceful Means: Peace and Conflict. *Development and Civilization*. Sage. https://doi.org/10.4135/9781446221631

Haar, R. J., Wang, K., Venters, H., Salonen, S., Patel, R., Nelson, T., Mishori, R., & Parmar, P. K. (2019). Documentation of Human Rights Abuses Among Rohingya Refugees from Myanmar. *Conflict and Health, 13*(1), 42. https://doi.org/10.1186/s13031-019-0226-9

Human Rights Watch. (2013). *'All You Can Do Is Pray': Crimes Against Humanity and Ethnic Cleansing of Rohingya Muslims in Burma's Arakan State* (ISBN: 978-1-62313-0053). H. R. Watch.

Kelly, L. (1987). The Continuum of Sexual Violence. In J. Hanmer & M. Maynard (Eds.), *Women, Violence and Social Control* (pp. 46–60). Palgrave Macmillan UK. https://doi.org/10.1007/978-1-349-18592-4_4

Kostovicova, D., Bojicic-Dzelilovic, V., & Henry, M. (2020). Drawing on the Continuum: A War and Post-War Political Economy of Gender-Based Violence in Bosnia and Herzegovina. *International Feminist Journal of Politics, 22*(2), 250–272. https://doi.org/10.1080/14616742.2019.1692686

McKay, M., & Win, K. C. (2018). Myanmar's Gender Paradox. *Anthropology Today, 34*(1), 1–3. https://doi.org/10.1111/1467-8322.12401

Morgan, K., & Björkert, S. T. (2006). I'd Rather You'd Lay Me on the Floor and Start Kicking Me': Understanding Symbolic Violence in Everyday Life. *Women's Studies International Forum, 29*(5), 441–452. https://doi.org/10.1016/j.wsif.2006.07.002

Office of the United Nations High Commissioner for Human Rights. (2019, September 9–27). *Sexual and Gender-Based Violence in Myanmar and the Gendered Impact of Its Ethnic Conflicts, Office of the United Nations High Commissioner for Human Rights*. Human Rights Council Forty second session. Agenda item4.

UN IIMM. (2024). Anti-Rohingya Hate Speech on Facebook: Content and Network Analysis, UN. chrome-extension://efaidnbmnnnibpcajpcglclefindmkaj/https://iimm.un.org/wp-content/uploads/2024/03/Hate-Speech-Report_EN.pdf

UNHCR. (2023, October 10). *Refugee Data Finder* UNHCR. Retrieved December 14, 2023, from https://www.unhcr.org/refugee-statistics/

United Nations. (2014). *Sexual Violence: a Tool of War*. Outreach Programme on the Rwanda Genocide and the United Nations, Issue. T. D. o. P. Information. https://www.un.org/en/preventgenocide/rwanda/assets/pdf/Backgrounder%20Sexual%20Violence%202014.pdf

Open Access This chapter is licensed under the terms of the Creative Commons Attribution 4.0 International License (http://creativecommons.org/licenses/by/4.0/), which permits use, sharing, adaptation, distribution and reproduction in any medium or format, as long as you give appropriate credit to the original author(s) and the source, provide a link to the Creative Commons license and indicate if changes were made.

The images or other third party material in this chapter are included in the chapter's Creative Commons license, unless indicated otherwise in a credit line to the material. If material is not included in the chapter's Creative Commons license and your intended use is not permitted by statutory regulation or exceeds the permitted use, you will need to obtain permission directly from the copyright holder.

CHAPTER 2

Gender, Violence, and Vulnerabilities in Forced Migration: A Multi-dimensional Approach

Abstract Violence is intertwined with a gendered logic, encompassing physical, sexual, structural, cultural, and symbolic dimensions. However, this association becomes even more complex within the context of refugees and forced migration. This chapter delves into the conceptual and theoretical framework surrounding multidimensional gendered vulnerabilities and violence in the context of forced migration. It explores key concepts integral to my discussion, including Galtung's conceptualisations of violence (direct, structural, and cultural violence), Bourdieu's theory of symbolic violence, and sexual and gender-based violence (SGBV) and vulnerabilities. Additionally, this chapter examines intersectionality and the continuum of violence framework to deepen our understanding of gendered vulnerabilities and violence in forced migration contexts.

Keywords Structural and cultural violence • Symbolic violence • Intersectionality • Continuum of violence

Introduction

Forced migrants frequently contend with a spectrum of challenges, vulnerabilities, and encounters with violence, including sexual violence. Vulnerabilities and violence transpire across diverse phases of displacement, commencing with the initial crisis that forces individuals to seek

© The Author(s) 2024
M. M. Salehin, *Gendered Vulnerabilities and Violence in Forced Migration*, https://doi.org/10.1007/978-3-031-62435-3_2

11

refuge and extending to the adversities during transit as well as within host locations. Yet, the types of violence and vulnerabilities faced by forced migrants, such as the Rohingya, also vary. Moreover, the experiences of violence and vulnerability, are not uniform and can differ based on the specific circumstances of their country of origin and the country to which they are forced to migrate. The violence and vulnerabilities that forced migrants face are gendered. Forced displacement exacerbates existing gender inequalities, rendering women, girls, and sexual minorities particularly vulnerable to exploitation, discrimination, trafficking, domestic and intimate partner violence, and sexual violence. Gendered vulnerabilities are also embedded into the structure, norms, and culture of the society that shapes violence, both in the private and in the public sphere. However, much of the existing research lacks a multi-dimensional approach to understanding the intersecting nature of gendered forms of violence experienced by forced migrants, including direct, structural, and symbolic violence. For example, in the context of migration, some academics focus on the continuum of violence (Cockburn, 2004; Kostovicova et al., 2020; Phillimore et al., 2023; Phillimore et al., 2022; Yadav & Horn, 2021), intersectionality (Reilly et al., 2022; Stavrevska & Smith, 2020; Tastsoglou et al., 2022), or structural and symbolic violence (Cross Riddle, 2017; Hourani et al., 2021). However, violence, whether physical, sexual, structural, cultural, or symbolic, is associated with a gendered logic. This association becomes more intricate in the context of refugees and forced migration. Therefore, considering the complexity inherent in forced migration, violence, and gender, I combine different approaches to get a nuanced understanding of the gendered nature of violence experienced by the forced migrant.

The objective of this chapter is to offer an overview of the conceptual and theoretical framework of multidimensional gendered vulnerabilities and violence in the context of refugees and forced migration. The chapter elucidates and contextualises several crucial concepts utilised in this book. They include Galtung's (Galtung, 1969, 1990, 1996) conceptualisation of violence (direct, structural, and cultural violence), Bourdieu's symbolic violence (Bourdieu, 1979; Bourdieu & Wacquant, 1992), and sexual and gender-based violence (SGBV) and vulnerabilities. Additionally, it delves into the intersectionality (Cho et al., 2013; Crenshaw, 1991; Crenshaw, 2017b) and continuum of violence (Cockburn, 2004; Kelly, 1987; Krause, 2015) framework to gain a better understanding of gendered vulnerabilities and violence in the context of forced migration. This chapter also discusses how and why Johan Galtung's conceptualisation of violence is relevant for comprehending violence against the forcibly displaced Rohingya. In order to understand and analyse the gendered violence against the Rohingya, I not only apply Galtung's theory of violence, but also take into account the criticisms of his ideas.

GENDERED VULNERABILITIES, VIOLENCE, AND MIGRATION

Previous research has highlighted gender vulnerabilities and violence at various stages of migration. For instance, there has been an observed trend of an increase in pregnancy among Sub-Saharan African women migrants en route to Europe. Pregnancy is employed as a strategy to avoid repatriation, due to the misconception that giving birth in Spain automatically guarantees them the right to residence (Carling, 2007, p. 328). During irregular border crossings, both actual and attempted, women face violence, including sexual violence, perpetrated by multiple actors such as border guards, security and police forces, traffickers, and even individuals positioned as saviours, such as humanitarian actors, who are involved in different stages of irregular migration. In many instances, sexual violence results in unwanted pregnancies (Carpenter, 2006). This was also evident in research among the Rohingya women. Some studies reported a disproportionate number of deaths between male and female migrants while crossing the border (Pickering & Cochrane, 2013). Others have identified increased levels of domestic violence, including intimate partner violence, within refugee communities in host countries (Akhter & Kusakabe, 2014).

Recent research on LGBTQ asylum applicants has indicated that legal procedures do not necessarily prevent or eliminate fraudulent cases; instead, they turn into forms of legal violence. These processes operate as regulatory practices based on heteronormativity, subjecting LGBTQ asylum seekers to legal violence that has manifested 'in four ways: isolation and loneliness, prolonged uncertainty, mental vulnerability, and physical vulnerability' (Llewellyn, 2021, p. 202). Even when they arrive in the countries of destination, research has shown different forms of violence, including domestic violence, experienced by refugees and irregular migrants. For example, among the documented Rohingya refugees living in Bangladesh, there is an increased level of different types of violence, including sexual and domestic violence (Akhter & Kusakabe, 2014).

Sexual and Gender-Based Violence (SGBV)

One of the various types of gendered vulnerabilities is sexual and gender-based violence (SGBV). Forced migration can heighten the risks of SGBV due to the increased vulnerabilities of displaced populations—including refugees, asylum seekers, and internally displaced persons—who may confront multiple and intersecting forms of discrimination based on factors such as gender, age, ethnicity, and sexual orientation. SGBV in forced migration can manifest in numerous ways, including sexual assault, rape, early and forced marriage, trafficking, and other forms of exploitation. Women, girls, and sexual minorities are particularly susceptible to SGBV and may face additional risks due to their gender or sexual orientation.

Gender-based violence (GBV) can be defined as:

> an umbrella term for any harmful act that is perpetrated against a person's will and that is based on socially ascribed (i.e. gender) differences between males and females. It includes acts that inflict physical, sexual or mental harm or suffering, threats of such acts, coercion, and other deprivations of liberty. These acts can occur in public or in private. Acts of GBV violate a number of universal human rights protected by international instruments and conventions. (Inter-Agency Standing Committee, 2015, p. 5)

SGBV has been used as a tool in war and conflict throughout history. Most frequently, rape has been used as a weapon of war (Gallimore, 2008; United Nations, 2014). Women and girl children have been almost exclusively targeted for SGBV. According to a recent UNHCR (2023) report, forcibly displaced and stateless women and girls are confronted with a heightened risk of gender-based violence, which now affects over 43 million individuals. Additionally, one in five forcibly displaced women experiences sexual violence, with the risk of intimate partner violence (IPV) increasing by 20 percent among this population. In the case of Rohingya refugees in Cox's Bazar, a recent report suggests that a significant proportion of women (57 percent) have been physically assaulted. Moreover, 22 percent of women have been denied access to resources, opportunities, and services by their domestic partners. Some women reported instances of psychological or emotional abuse, while others experienced rape (2 percent) and sexual assault (16 percent) (International Rescue Committee, 2020).

Ozcurumez et al. (2021) conducted a review of the literature on SGBV in forced migration from 1993 to 2018 and found three trends in gender and forced migration research. The first trend focuses on the experiences of refugee women, men, youth, the elderly, the disabled, and LGBTQ individuals, although this group of researchers rarely focuses on the fluidity and consequences, both long and short term, of such experiences. The second group of researchers focuses on the male refugees who have been described as 'perpetrators of violence and discrimination; as powerful gatekeepers and potential allies; and as emasculated troublemakers' while women have been described as victims. Skjelsbæk (2001) classifies this line of research as 'essentialist'. The third variant of research focuses on the 'consequences of forced migration and internal displacement in Africa, the Middle East and the Balkans as case studies, ethno-political conflicts, terrorism and wars, rather than following the process of migration from displacement to settlement/protracted displacement' (Ozcurumez et al., 2021, p. 75). To broaden the horizon, they propose to 'encompass different spatial and territorial private and public experiences from reception centres to urban settlements' in the conceptualisation of SGBV in forced migration (Ozcurumez et al., 2021, p. 67). This in turn would facilitate a more integrated policy approach to addressing its consequences for all, including migrants, their families and different service providers. In this book, I explain the different forms of violence experienced by the Rohingya forced migrants, including direct, structural, cultural, and symbolic violence, and elucidate how they are gendered.

STRUCTURAL, CULTURAL, AND SYMBOLIC VIOLENCE

Definitions of violence are often contested and ambiguous. 'Violence' normally connotes four major elements: (a) an identifiable actor or groups of actors, (b) an identifiable physical action, (c) a clear harm psychological or physical or both, and (d) an identifiable victim (Brunk, 2012, p. 17).

For Galtung (1996, p. 197) violence is 'avoidable insults to basic human needs and more generally to life, lowering the real level of needs satisfaction below what is potentially possible. Threats of violence are also violence'. He defined three types of violence: personal/direct violence, structural/indirect violence, and cultural violence. The first, personal or direct violence, is a type of violence where there is an identifiable actor that commits the violence. When we think of violence, we often tend to think about direct violence. Direct[1] or personal violence refers to the physical and psychological harm or damage caused by individuals or groups towards other individuals or groups. This includes actions such as physical assault, murder, war, and terrorism, wherein there is a clear and immediate perpetrator who inflicts harm on others. Yet, Galtung's most significant contribution to the understanding of violence is the development of the concept of 'structural violence'. Structural violence is a form of violence in which there is no identifiable perpetrator of the violence, it is rather 'built into the structure and shows up as unequal power and consequently as unequal life chances' (Galtung, 1969, p. 171). One major challenge for this concept is that structural violence is subtle and often goes unrecognised.

Twenty years after the introduction of structural violence, Galtung introduced the concept of 'cultural violence' which includes 'those aspects of culture, the symbolic sphere of our existence—exemplified by religion and ideology, language and art, empirical science and formal science (logic, mathematics)—that can be used to justify or legitimize direct or structural violence' (Galtung (1990, p. 291). Galtung presents these three types of violence in a triangular form where violence can start at any corner of the triangle and be easily transmitted to the other corners. 'With the violent structure institutionalized and the violent culture internalized, direct violence also tends to become institutionalized, repetitive, ritualistic, like a vendetta' (Galtung, 1990, p. 302). Galtung's conceptualisation of structural and cultural violence has some similarities with Bourdieu (1979) notion of 'symbolic violence'. Both theories provided valuable insights into the nature and forms of violence, but they each offer unique perspectives and focus on different aspects of violence.

Symbolic violence, 'to put it as tersely and simply as possible, is the *violence which is exercised upon a social agent with his or her complicity'* (Bourdieu & Wacquant, 1992, p. 167, emphasis in original). Symbolic violence operates through 'symbolic systems', such as language and cultural practices through which the dominant groups impose values and norms onto others in a manner that leads the targeted group to internalise what is referred to as legitimate knowledge, thus perpetuating the existing social order. As Bourdieu (1979, pp. 80-81) puts it, 'the dominant fractions, whose power is based on economic and political capital, seek to impose the legitimacy of their domination either through their own symbolic production (discourse, writings, etc.) or through the intermediary of conservative ideologists who serve the interests of the dominant fractions—but only incidentally'. In symbolic violence, power, social hierarchies, and inequalities are produced and sustained not primarily through physical force but rather through various forms of symbolic domination. Yet, hierarchies and systems of domination persist when both those in power (dominant) and those subjected to power (dominated) view these systems as legitimate. In this context, legitimacy relies on consent, complicity, and misrecognition (Morgan & Björkert, 2006; Thapar-Björkert et al., 2016). Consequently, individuals on both sides think and act in alignment with their perceived best interests within the framework of the system (Schubert, 2014). 'Hierarchies and systems of domination are then reproduced to the extent that the dominant and the dominated perceive these systems to be legitimate, and thus think and act in their own best interests within the context of the system itself' (Schubert, 2014, p. 182).

Here, social agents could misrecognise violence, meaning they do not perceive it as such and think it is natural. As Bourdieu and Wacquant (2004, p. 172) put it, '"recognition," then, is the set of fundamental, prereflexive assumptions that social agents engage by the mere fact of taking the world for granted, of accepting the world as it is, and of finding it natural because *their mind is constructed according to cognitive structures that are issued out of very structures of the world*' (emphasis in original). Gendered violence is an example of such symbolic violence in which women are taught and socialised to regard themselves as less intelligent, unreliable, incapable, etc. and their lives can be hence dominated and controlled. As a result, men's dominance over women, or any violence rooted in patriarchy, may be felt as 'natural' and go unchallenged. For example, instances of wife-beating and men's multiple marriages among the Rohingya could be regarded as symbolic violence, wherein women, despite being victims of spousal bodily violence, express that they never felt insulted by their husbands' actions. Although much academic research and many non-academic reports exist on direct violence against the Rohingya (e.g., killings, murder, torture, and rape), research is scarce on how unequal power relations, traditional gender norms, a patriarchal social structure, marginalisation and inequitable access to resources and services—including justice, and hate speech and Islamophobia against the Rohingya results in structural, cultural, and symbolic violence.

Both symbolic violence and cultural violence are valuable concepts for comprehending the nature of violence. In both cases, Galtung's (1990) cultural violence and Bourdieu's (1979) symbolic violence can make direct and structural violence look and feel natural. Also, both conceptualisations share a common focus: the insidious and invisible nature of violence. In the case of cultural violence, as argued by Galtung, it is 'used to legitimize violence in its direct or structural form' (Galtung, 1990, p. 291). Bourdieu regards symbolic violence as instruments used to legitimise the 'domination of one class over another' (Bourdieu, 1979, p. 80). Yet, one relevant distinction is that Bourdieu's theory places a strong emphasis on power relations and the ways in which dominant groups use symbolic violence to maintain their dominance. Galtung's theory, while acknowledging power imbalances as a form of structural violence, does not focus as explicitly on the dynamics of power. Another interesting point is that, while Galtung's theory of violence has been criticised for the lack of a gender perspective, Bourdieu's concept of symbolic violence has been used more extensively in feminist theory. This is because symbolic violence can help explain how gender inequalities are reproduced and legitimised in everyday practices and common understandings.

Gender in Structural, Symbolic, and Cultural Violence

My research focused on all four types of violence as they were experienced by Rohingya women and men. Direct or personal violence is the most visible one, while structural violence and cultural and symbolic violence are not. The primary distinction between the two forms of violence is in how they manifest and are sustained. Structural violence is generally carried out through societal structures and institutions, whereas symbolic violence is maintained by individuals who have internalised societal norms and expectations. Despite their differences, both types of violence play a role in perpetuating gender violence and are often deeply interconnected. In my research, I explore how and why the Myanmar military and the ultranationalist Buddhists have used cultural logic to justify direct and structural violence. I applied the concept of structural violence to my analysis of how differentiated access to power and resources (social, economic, political) intersects with gender and sexual identity, ethnicity, and class position to produce vulnerabilities and violence against the Rohingya. Galtung's theory of violence, while addressing direct, structural, and cultural violence, does not explicitly consider how these forms of violence are influenced by gender. Although Galtung's violence triangle offers a 'unified framework within which all violence can be seen', his theory needs to 'incorporate notions of gender as a social construct' (Confortini, 2006, p. 333) to comprehend the complexity inherent in the nature of violence. Thus, Confortini (2006) argues that Galtung's theory of violence could be enhanced by considering gender as a social construct embedded with power dynamics, rather than equating it with biological sex. It is imperative to acknowledge that the various social categories that shape our understanding of the world are deeply influenced by gender and are implicated in the reproduction of violence. Violence can, therefore, produce and define 'gender identities and, in turn, is produced and defined by them' (Confortini 2006, p. 333). Confortini argues that violence plays a significant role in constructing and sustaining gender relations, particularly in the context of hegemonic masculinity. Galtung's main point, as Cockburn (2004, p. 30) argues, 'prompts us to look again at male-dominant gender relations. Long before a man uses physical violence against a woman, she may experience "structural violence" in a marriage in which her husband or a constraining patriarchal community holds power over her'. Gendered violence and male domination, as Bourdieu argues, is an example of symbolic violence (Bourdieu & Wacquant, 2004) where the dominance of men is legitimated as the natural 'order of things' and in which women are 'consigned to inferior social positions' (Bourdieu & Wacquant, 1992, pp. 168, 173).

STRUCTURAL VIOLENCE, INTERSECTIONALITY AND THE CONTINUUM OF VIOLENCE

There is still limited research that delves into the frameworks and mechanisms responsible for generating particular gender-related vulnerabilities for refugees. Some research tends to focus on SGBV in forced migration as a source or push factor in migration and thus can overlook various other manifestations of gender-based violence (GBV) against migrants or those associated with migration. Moreover, these studies may also fail to recognise links between different forms of GBV and their underlying structural and systematic inequalities in the forms of the structural, cultural, and symbolic violence that refugees experience at the different stages and processes of migration (Freedman et al., 2022). In my research, I explored the different forms of violence (direct, structural, cultural and symbolic) experienced by Rohingya forced migrants at different stages, both in the country of origin (Myanmar) and in the country of destination (Bangladesh). To address this, I asked the question presented by Jakobsen (2014), 'What's gendered about gender-based violence' in the refugee and forced migration context?' I also applied intersectionality as a conceptual framework to understand the violence and gendered vulnerabilities of the Rohingya refugees. A comprehensive analysis of the vulnerabilities and insecurities experienced by forced migrant women necessitates a deeper exploration of the current crisis. Intersectionality, as coined by Crenshaw (1989), a US critical legal race scholar, emphasises that violence and oppression against women of colour originates from multiple systems of oppression and inequalities. In a recent interview, Crenshaw (2017a) said,

> Intersectionality is a lens through which you can see where power comes and collides, where it interlocks and intersects. It's not simply that there's a race problem here, a gender problem here, and a class or LBGTQ problem there. Many times that framework erases what happens to people who are subject to all of these things.

I used intersectionality as an analytical tool to explore the experience of oppression and violence by the Rohingya refugees, based on multiple intersecting axes of social division, in particular race, religion, ethnicity, language, age, gender, and class (Reilly et al., 2022; Stavrevska & Smith, 2020). As Crenshaw (1989, p. 140) argues, any analysis that does not take intersectionality into account fails to adequately capture the particular manner and ways in which any ethnic, sexual and gendered minority group is subordinated. Applying an intersectional viewpoint to migration and refugee studies encourages a nuanced comprehension of the vulnerabilities and subordinate positions of migrants and refugees. This involves acknowledging diverse forms of precarious situations arising from elements like immigration status, unpaid labour, unstable employment, the perpetuation of stereotypes and biases about women refugees, the racial background of refugees, the age and skills of the refugees, etc.

In this research, I explored the intersectionality of the cultural and structural dimensions of violence. As Cross Riddle (2017) says, 'just as structural violence situates harm in a matrix of social forces, intersectionality situates women's life experiences in a "matrix of domination"'. The concept of intersectionality provides a more comprehensive understanding of how a structure functions in social dynamics. It elucidates how the accumulation of various social identities (gender, religion, sexuality, ethnicity, etc.) can act as a barrier, impeding individuals from accessing spaces, knowledge, and fundamental human rights. Yet, intersectionality theory, while providing valuable insights into the complexities of violence and peace, has been criticised for its absence in practice, its focus on multiple identities at the expense of broader structural factors, its complexity, the risk of essentialism, and potential Western biases (Salem, 2018).

In addition to intersectionality and the concepts of violence propagated by Galtung and Bourdieu, I also employed the concept of the 'continuum of violence'. This approach allowed me to comprehend the experiences of violence among the Rohingya, examining how gendered vulnerabilities persist from the conflict zone to the so-called safe zone. My objective was to comprehend violence within the context of history, prevailing social and institutional structures, and the experiences in their country of origin (Myanmar). This understanding extends to their so-called safe destination (Bangladesh) across different time periods, forms, and scales of violence. Many academics have analysed violence as a continuum, in particular gendered violence (Cockburn, 2004; Kelly, 1987; Kostovicova et al., 2020; Krause, 2015; Phillimore et al., 2023; Phillimore et al., 2022; Yadav & Horn, 2021).

Through the 'continuum of violence' we can understand how different forms of sexual and gender-based violence in forced migration are 'connected across scope, forms, and conditions of violence and throughout conflict, flight, and displacement' (Phillimore et al., 2022, p. 2208). It is an important way to see violence through its temporal dimensions (i.e., pre-, during and post-refugee journeys), locational dimensions (i.e., bedroom, home, street to the battlefield), scalar dimensions (i.e., personal to international), and through the forms it takes (i.e., structural/cultural violence legitimising direct violence) (Cockburn, 2004).

I investigated gender violence against the Rohingya by engaging with the intersectional nature of the continuums of violence. This effort involved examining how various dimensions of social division—such as race, ethnicity, class, age, religion, gender, and sexualities—contribute to different experiences of violence in different time periods, forms, and scales. This endeavour recognised the institutionalisation and legitimisation of structural inequality and gendered power relations, or more broadly, structural violence.

Conclusion

Understanding and analysing gender violence in the context of forced migration requires a multi-dimensional approach that takes into account the complex ways in which social categories, statuses, and structures of power and oppression interact to result in, what Galtung referred to as, direct or structural violence. Forced migrants—in my case, the Rohingya—are often subjected to interconnected structural and symbolic violence throughout different stages of their journey as forced migrants, from their country of origin through their transit to their country of destination. Gendered violence, including sexual violence, explicitly demonstrates how structural and symbolic violence manifests an interconnection in all stages of forced migration. Therefore, it is imperative to view the various forms of gendered violence experienced by refugees as part of a continuum where women and men encounter different forms and scales of violence. For instance, a woman who was raped by the military in Myanmar continued to face trauma upon reaching Bangladesh, along with the social stigma associated with it. If these same women become victims of violence by their partners, the existing community structure could potentially ostracise them. Differentiated and limited access to resources makes it difficult for women to seek and obtain formal justice. In the subsequent chapters, I will illustrate how I applied the concepts discussed in this chapter.

NOTE

1. For Galtung (1969, p. 168), Direct violence is related to 'somatic incapacitation, or deprivation of health, alone (with killing as the extreme form), at the hands of an actor who intends this to be the consequence'.
   See: Galtung, J. (1969). Violence, Peace, and Peace Research. *Journal of Peace Research*, 6(3), 167–191. http://www.jstor.org/stable/422690, ibid.

REFERENCES

Akhter, S., & Kusakabe, K. (2014). Gender-based Violence among Documented Rohingya Refugees in Bangladesh. *Indian Journal of Gender Studies, 21*(2), 225–246. https://doi.org/10.1177/0971521514525088

Bourdieu, P. (1979). Symbolic Power. *Critique of Anthropology, 4*(13–14), 77–85. https://doi.org/10.1177/0308275x7900401307

Bourdieu, P., & Wacquant, L. (2004). Symbolic Violence. In N. Scheper-Hughes & P. Bourgois (Eds.), *Violence in War and Peace: An Anthology* (pp. 271–274). Wiley-Blackwell.

Bourdieu, P., & Wacquant, L. J. D. (1992). *An Invitation to Reflexive Sociology*. Polity Press.

Brunk, C. G. (2012). Shaping a Vision: The Nature of Peace Studies. In C. P. Webel & J. Johansen (Eds.), *Peace and Conflict Studies: A Reader* (pp. 10–24). Routledge.

Carling, J. (2007). Migration Control and Migrant Fatalities at the Spanish-African Borders. *International Migration Review, 41*(2), 316–343.

Carpenter, J. (2006). The gender of control. In S. Pickering & L. Weber (Eds.), *Borders, Mobility and Technologies of Control*. Springer.

Cho, S., Crenshaw, K. W., & McCall, L. (2013). Toward a Field of Intersectionality Studies: Theory, Applications, and Praxis. *Signs: Journal of Women in Culture and Society, 38*(4), 785–810. https://doi.org/10.1086/669608

Cockburn, C. (2004). The Continuum of Violence: A Gender Perspective on War and Peace. In W. Giles (Ed.), *Sites of Violence: Gender and Conflict Zones* (p. 0). University of California Press. https://doi.org/10.1525/california/9780520230729.003.0002

Confortini, C. C. (2006). Galtung, Violence, and Gender: The Case for a Peace Studies/Feminism Alliance. *Peace & Change, 31*(3), 333–367. https://doi.org/10.1111/j.1468-0130.2006.00378.x

Crenshaw, K. (1989). Demarginalizing the Intersection of Race and Sex: A Black Feminist Critique of Antidiscrimination Doctrine, Feminist Theory and Antiracist Politics. *University of Chicago Legal Forum, 1989*(1), 29.

Crenshaw, K. (1991). Mapping the Margins: Intersectionality, Identity Politics, and Violence against Women of Color. *Stanford Law Review, 43*(6), 1241–1299. https://doi.org/10.2307/1229039

Crenshaw, K. (2017a, June 8). *Kimberlé Crenshaw on Intersectionality, More than Two Decades Later* [Interview]. https://www.law.columbia.edu/news/archive/kimberle-crenshaw-intersectionality-more-two-decades-later, accessed on May 27, 2020.

Crenshaw, K. (2017b). *On intersectionality: Essential writings*. The New Press.

Cross Riddle, K. (2017). Structural Violence, Intersectionality, and Justpeace: Evaluating Women's Peacebuilding Agency in Manipur, India. *Hypatia, 32*(3), 574–592. https://doi.org/10.1111/hypa.12340

Freedman, J., Sahraoui, N., & Tastsoglou, E. (2022). Thinking about Gender and Violence in Migration: An Introduction. In N. S. Jane Freedman & E. Tastsoglou (Eds.), *Gender-Based Violence in Migration: Interdisciplinary, Feminist and Intersectional Approaches* (pp. 3–28). Palgrave Macmillan.

Gallimore, R. B. (2008). Militarism, Ethnicity, and Sexual Violence in the Rwandan Genocide. *Feminist Africa, 10*, 9–30. https://www.jstor.org/stable/48725951

Galtung, J. (1969). Violence, Peace, and Peace Research. *Journal of Peace Research, 6*(3), 167–191. http://www.jstor.org/stable/422690

Galtung, J. (1990). Cultural Violence. *Journal of Peace Research, 27*(3), 291–305. https://doi.org/10.1177/0022343390027003005

Galtung, J. (1996). *Peace by Peaceful Means: Peace and Conflict, Development and Civilization*. Sage. https://doi.org/10.4135/9781446221631.

Hourani, J., Block, K., Phillimore, J., Bradby, H., Ozcurumez, S., Goodson, L., & Vaughan, C. (2021). Structural and Symbolic Violence Exacerbates the Risks and Consequences of Sexual and Gender-Based Violence for Forced Migrant

Women. *Frontiers in Human Dynamics, 3.* https://doi.org/10.3389/fhumd.2021.769611

Inter-Agency Standing Committee. (2015). *Guidelines for Integrating Gender-Based Violence Interventions in Humanitarian Action: Reducing Risk, Promoting Resilience and Aiding Recovery.* I.-A. S. Committee. https://gbvguidelines.org/en/

International Rescue Committee. (2020). *The Shadow Pandemic: Gender-Based Violence among Rohingya Refugees in Cox's Bazar.* https://www.rescue.org/sites/default/files/document/2247/theshadowpandemicbangladesh.pdf, accessed on September 25, 2021.

Jakobsen, H. (2014). What's Gendered about Gender-Based Violence? An Empirically Grounded Theoretical Exploration from Tanzania. *Gender & Society, 28*(4), 537–561. https://doi.org/10.1177/0891243214532311

Kelly, L. (1987). The Continuum of Sexual Violence. In J. Hanmer & M. Maynard (Eds.), *Women, Violence and Social Control* (pp. 46–60). Palgrave Macmillan UK. https://doi.org/10.1007/978-1-349-18592-4_4

Kostovicova, D., Bojicic-Dzelilovic, V., & Henry, M. (2020). Drawing on the Continuum: A War and Post-War Political Economy of Gender-Based Violence in Bosnia and Herzegovina. *International Feminist Journal of Politics, 22*(2), 250–272. https://doi.org/10.1080/14616742.2019.1692686

Krause, U. (2015). A Continuum of Violence? Linking Sexual and Gender-Based Violence During Conflict, Flight, and Encampment. *Refugee Survey Quarterly, 34*(4), 1–19. https://doi.org/10.1093/rsq/hdv014

Llewellyn, C. (2021). Captive While Waiting to Be Free: Legal Violence and LGBTQ Asylum Applicant Experiences in the USA. *Sexuality Research and Social Policy, 18*(1), 202–212. https://doi.org/10.1007/s13178-020-00449-7

Morgan, K., & Björkert, S. T. (2006). I'd Rather You'd Lay Me on the Floor and Start Kicking Me': Understanding Symbolic Violence in Everyday Life. *Women's Studies International Forum, 29*(5), 441–452. https://doi.org/10.1016/j.wsif.2006.07.002

Ozcurumez, S., Akyuz, S., & Bradby, H. (2021). The Conceptualization Problem in Research and Responses to Sexual and Gender-Based Violence in Forced Migration. *Journal of Gender Studies, 30*(1), 66–78. https://doi.org/10.1080/09589236.2020.1730163

Phillimore, J., Block, K., Bradby, H., Ozcurumez, S., & Papoutsi, A. (2023). Forced Migration, Sexual and Gender-Based Violence and Integration: Effects, Risks and Protective Factors. *Journal of International Migration and Integration, 24*(2), 715–745. https://doi.org/10.1007/s12134-022-00970-1

Phillimore, J., Pertek, S., Akyuz, S., Darkal, H., Hourani, J., McKnight, P., Ozcurumez, S., & Taal, S. (2022). 'We Are Forgotten': Forced Migration,

Sexual and Gender-Based Violence, and Coronavirus Disease-2019. *Violence Against Women, 28*(9), 2204–2230. https://doi.org/10.1177/1077801 2211030943

Pickering, S., & Cochrane, B. (2013). Irregular border-crossing deaths and gender: Where, how and why women die crossing borders. *Theoretical Criminology, 17*(1), 27–48.

Reilly, N., Bjørnholt, M., & Tastsoglou, E. (2022). Vulnerability, Precarity and Intersectionality: A Critical Review of Three Key Concepts for Understanding Gender-Based Violence in Migration Contexts. In J. Freedman, N. Sahraoui, & E. Tastsoglou (Eds.), *Gender-Based Violence in Migration: Interdisciplinary, Feminist and Intersectional Approaches* (pp. 29–56). Springer International Publishing. https://doi.org/10.1007/978-3-031-07929-0_2

Salem, S. (2018). Intersectionality and Its Discontents: Intersectionality as Traveling Theory. *The European Journal of Women's Studies, 25*(4), 403–418. https://doi.org/10.1177/1350506816643999

Schubert, J. D. (2014). Suffering/Symbolic Violence. In M. Grenfell (Ed.), *Pierre Bourdieu: Key Concepts* (pp. 183–198). Acumen. http://ebookcentral.proquest.com/lib/tromsoub-ebooks/detail.action?docID=3060927

Skjelsbæk, I. (2001). Sexual Violence and War: Mapping Out a Complex Relationship. *European Journal of International Relations, 7*(2), 211–237. https://doi.org/10.1177/1354066101007002003

Stavrevska, E. B., & Smith, S. (2020). Intersectionality and Peace. In *The Palgrave Encyclopedia of Peace and Conflict Studies* (pp. 1–8). Springer International Publishing. https://doi.org/10.1007/978-3-030-11795-5_120-1

Tastsoglou, E., Sahraoui, N., & Freedman, J. (2022). *Gender-Based Violence in Migration: Interdisciplinary, Feminist and Intersectional Approaches* (1st 2022. ed.). Springer International Publishing: Imprint: Palgrave Macmillan.

Thapar-Björkert, S., Samelius, L., & Sanghera, G. S. (2016). Exploring Symbolic Violence in the Everyday: Misrecognition, Condescension. *Consent and Complicity. Feminist Review, 112*(1), 144–162. https://doi.org/10.1057/fr.2015.53

UNHCR. (2023). *UNHCR Global Appeal 2023.* UNHCR. https://reporting.unhcr.org/globalappeal2023/pdf?page=37, accessed on April 29, 2023.

United Nations. (2014). *Sexual Violence: a Tool of War* (Outreach Programme on the Rwanda Genocide and the United Nations, Issue. T. D. o. P. Information. https://www.un.org/en/preventgenocide/rwanda/assets/pdf/Backgrounder%20Sexual%20Violence%202014.pdf

Yadav, P., & Horn, D. M. (2021). CONTINUUMS OF VIOLENCE: Feminist Peace Research and Gender-Based Violence. In T. Väyrynen, S. Parashar, É. Féron, & C. C. Confortini (Eds.), *Routledge Handbook of Feminist Peace Research.* Routledge. https://www.routledgehandbooks.com/doi/10.432 4/9780429024160-12

Open Access This chapter is licensed under the terms of the Creative Commons Attribution 4.0 International License (http://creativecommons.org/licenses/by/4.0/), which permits use, sharing, adaptation, distribution and reproduction in any medium or format, as long as you give appropriate credit to the original author(s) and the source, provide a link to the Creative Commons license and indicate if changes were made.

The images or other third party material in this chapter are included in the chapter's Creative Commons license, unless indicated otherwise in a credit line to the material. If material is not included in the chapter's Creative Commons license and your intended use is not permitted by statutory regulation or exceeds the permitted use, you will need to obtain permission directly from the copyright holder.

CHAPTER 3

The Rohingya Crisis: Background on Myanmar, the Current Conflict, and Relevant Actors

Abstract The chapter delves into the history behind the Rohingya crisis, tracing its roots beyond the events of 2017. Although the Myanmar government established the year 1824 as the cut-off date for citizenship, historical evidence suggests that the term 'Rohingya' was used prior to this period, indicating the longstanding presence of this Muslim minority group in the region. Furthermore, the chapter sheds light on the multifaceted nature of the crisis, involving actors such as the state, the military, Buddhist monks, and the Arakan Rohingya Salvation Army (ARSA). Of particular significance is the unlikely alliance formed between ultranationalist Buddhists and the military, who were once adversaries but joined forces against the Rohingya population, leading to intensified violence and displacement. This historical context provides crucial insights into the complexities and underlying factors driving the ongoing Rohingya crisis.

Keywords History • Military • Ultranationalist Buddhists • ARSA • Ma Ba Tha

INTRODUCTION

The origin of the 2017 forced displacement of the Rohingya into Bangladesh, while part of a long history of persecution, can be traced back to 2012, when violence erupted following rumours about the alleged rape

© The Author(s) 2024
M. M. Salehin, *Gendered Vulnerabilities and Violence in Forced Migration*, https://doi.org/10.1007/978-3-031-62435-3_3

of a Buddhist woman by three Muslim Rohingya men. Subsequent years witnessed intermittent violence and hate speech against the Rohingya until the crisis reached its climax in August 2017. The complexity of the Rohingya crisis is linked to the historical development of Rohingya identity and their presence in Myanmar. While international organisations recognise the self-identification of the Rohingya, Myanmar consistently rejects the notion of Rohingya identity, instead branding them as illegal immigrants from Bangladesh. In contrast, the Rohingya assert that their historical presence in Myanmar dates back several centuries, when they arrived via sea routes as primarily traders, warriors, and saints. The roots of the crisis extend beyond the British colonial period, which impacted the Indian subcontinent, including Myanmar (then called Burma). However, the post-independence Burman state and its policies on indigeneity played a more pivotal role. Although British rule played a role in the creation of the crisis, the politics of the independent Burman state regarding indigeneity played a larger role. Of significance is the narrative that differentiated the Buddhist Burmese (us) from the Rohingya (them) and the rise of ultranationalist Buddhists. This chapter provides a succinct exploration of the historical backdrop to the ongoing Rohingya crisis. It further examines the multitude of actors involved in the conflict and elucidates the intricate complexities between the state, the military, and the monks in Myanmar.

BACKGROUND TO THE ROHINGYA CRISIS

Although there is not a consensus, it is generally accepted that the term 'Rohingya' is composed of *Rohang* (Arakan) and *Ga* or *Gya* (from), meaning that the Rohingya are people who originated from Arakan (now Rakhine State of Myanmar) (Albert & Maizland, 2020). However, the term is controversial. The people call themselves Rohingya and the ethnonym is widely used by the international community, including the United Nations, but the Myanmar government and the majority of the population of Myanmar consider them as illegal Bengali migrants from neighbouring Bangladesh (Kipgen, 2013, p. 300).

The current Rohingya crisis has its roots in the era of British rule when colonial census-takers first classified people according to 'national' and 'tribal' identities. When Burma gained independence, the Constitution of the Union of Burma (1948) granted citizenship to individuals born in Burma who had at least one grandparent of a 'native race' (*taing-yin-tha*) as well as those born and residing in British dominions for at least eight years (Kyaw, 2019). However, the first citizenship law, the Union Citizenship Act of 1948, did not name the Rohingya as one of the country's 'native races' (Parashar & Alam, 2019), and the military regime's Citizenship Law of 1982 failed to recognise the Rohingya as an ethnic group with ties to Myanmar prior to 1824, when Arakan (Rakhine State) came under British occupation. This cut-off date for citizenship primarily resembles the dominant narrative inside Myanmar that 'Rohingya' is a recent term, primarily associated with migration from British colonial India. Yet, many sources indicate that 'Rohingya' existed even before that. For example, Francis Buchanan, an East India Company employee, wrote about Muslims '...who have been long settled in *Arakan,* and who call themselves *Rooingya,* or natives of *Arakan*' (Buchanan, 1799, p. 237). During Buchanan's travel to South East Bengal, he found that the Chakmas and Saks of the eighteenth century called Arakan as 'Roang' (Van Schendel, 1992, p. 104). Additionally, Qnungo (1988) wrote that the word Rohingya came to exist in different forms and spelling.

In 1983, the Myanmar national census increased the available ethnic categories from 3 to 135. However, 'Rohingya' was not mentioned in it; 'Bengali' was used instead. By choosing the 'Bengali' identity, the Rohingya were in effect rendered stateless (Berlie, 2008), enabling systematic repression and forced migration. The first mass forced migration of the Rohingya from Myanmar (then Burma) to Bangladesh took place in the late 1970s. Approximately 200,000 Rohingya refugees fled to Bangladesh in 1978 when the military junta in Myanmar launched 'Operation Dragon King' as a way of '"protecting" the sanctity of Buddhism from the "foreign outliers" who posed a "threat"' (Akins, 2018). In 1979, most of the Rohingya refugees were forcibly repatriated back to Myanmar (Médecins Sans Frontières, 2002). The second mass forced migration occurred after the ruling State Law and Order Restoration Council (SLORC) in Myanmar failed to hand over power after the 'Multi-Party Democracy General Elections' in 1990. This provoked demonstrations by monks and students. The government felt it needed '"a scapegoat, a distraction and common enemy" to unite a disillusioned and angry populace' (Alam, 2019, p. 13) and chose the Rohingya for two reasons. Firstly, the monks already despised the Rohingya, and secondly, there was preexisting deep-rooted antagonistic sentiment by the majority Burmans against the Rohingya. Thus, distracting attention from the movement towards Rohingya was an effective strategy (Parashar & Alam, 2019). The result was that, in 1992, approximately 250,000 Rohingya took refuge in

Bangladesh when the SLORC increased its military presence and enacted compulsory labour, forced relocation, rape, executions, and torture on the Rohingya in northern Rakhine.

The most recent wave of violence against the Rohingya started in June 2012. On May 28, 2012, a Buddhist Rakhine woman was gang raped and murdered. The state media reported that the rapists were 'Muslims' and broadcasted different images of the murdered woman that went viral on social media (McCarthy & Menager, 2017). On May 29, three suspected Muslim men were arrested. In June, a crowd of some 300 Buddhist Arakanese stopped a Yangon-bound bus at Toungup township in Rakhine State. They took ten Muslim men off the bus and beat them to death. Following this incident, angry mobs from both Rakhine and Muslim communities went on the rampage, killing at least seven people, as per the official report (International Crisis Group, 2012). According to the state's press release, the June riots resulted in the deaths of 88 people—31 Rakhines and 57 Rohingya. However, the Equal Rights Trust (ERT), an international human rights organisation, claims the actual number of Rohingya deaths to be at least 650, with 1200 missing (Kipgen, 2013). The June riots caused the displacement of 75,000 people, mostly Rohingya (UNHCR, 2013). Later that year, in October, a new round of violence broke out in Rakhine state. According to Physicians for Human Rights, a Rakhine merchant was killed by a mob in Mrauk U township on October 21 after selling rice to a Muslim customer. In this context, it's crucial to emphasise that Buddhist monks have led a commercial boycott, presenting it as a religious obligation to incite widespread outrage against merchants deemed 'greedy' for trading with Muslims (The Economist, 2012). This portrayal of the boycott as a religious imperative serves to justify and garner backing for discriminatory measures against Rohingya Muslims, perpetuating cultural violence. Following October 21 mob violence, riots broke out in nine different townships for three days (Gittleman et al., 2013). According to Human Rights Watch, the October 2012 violence had been 'one-sided and systematic', and the attacks 'were organized, incited, and committed by local Arakanese political party operatives, the Buddhist monkhood, and ordinary Arakanese, at times directly supported by state security forces' (Human Rights Watch, 2013, p. 165; Republic of the Union of Myanmar, 2013).

Several hundred men, women, and children were killed, and entire Muslim neighbourhoods and villages were razed, by the Arakanese population. Human rights organisations estimate that intercommunal violence since mid-2012 displaced approximately 125,000 Rohingya and other Muslims and a smaller number of Arakanese people in Rakhine State (Human Rights Watch, 2013). However, of those arrested afterwards for committing violence during the June and October riots, the vast majority were Rohingya (849 out of a total 1121 arrests), and their charges were far more serious than those facing non-Muslim detainees. Other detainees also include Rakhine (233), and Hindu (27) (Gittleman et al., 2013, pp. 11–12).

The years following the 2012 conflict saw sporadic but significant incidences of violence against the Rohingya and other Muslims. For example, in 2013, several incidences of violence took place against Muslims throughout Myanmar, including the country's second largest city, Mandalay, and its former capital, Rangoon (Yangoon). On February 18, several hundred monks and Buddhist nationalists attacked Muslim schools and businesses in Rangoon and, on February 20, 13 Rohingya women and girls were beaten and gang-raped by the Nasaka (the Burmese security force) (Gittleman et al., 2013). It is, therefore, evident that multiple actors are involved in the conflict from the Myanmar side.

From the side of the Rohingya, it was the Arakan Rohingya Salvation Army (ARSA) who waged violence against the state security forces. *Harakah Al Yaqeen* (Faith Movement), currently known as the Arakan Rohingya Salvation Army (ARSA), is the militant organisation of the Rohingya. ARSA has claimed in its Twitter account[1] that it is an ethno-nationalist movement 'fighting for liberation of persecuted Rohingya'. The conflict between the Buddhists and Rohingya Muslims escalated further following ARSA's claim of responsibility for assaults on the Myanmar border posts in Rakhine State in October 2016, resulting in the deaths of nine border officers, four soldiers, and 69 ARSA members (BBC, 2016a; BBC, 2016b; Slodkowski, 2016).

Intermittent fighting between the Myanmar military (Tatmadaw) and ARSA continued throughout 2017. According to Myanmar government, ARSA killed around 44 Rohingya civilians and abducted 22 Rohingya in July in retaliatory strikes against individuals perceived as government collaborators by the ARSA members. However, ARSA refused the accusation (ASEAN Economist, 2017). On August 25, 2017, ARSA claimed responsibility for a series of coordinated attacks on more than 30 police and army posts (Head, 2017). The Suu Kyi government claimed that the attacks resulted in a death toll of 77 ARSA insurgents and 12 security force members in northern Maungdaw in Rakhine state (Aljazeera, 2017). On

September 24, 2017, Myanmar's military also accused ARSA of murdering 28 Hindus in the village of Ye Baw Kya in Rakhine State (AFP, 2017). The military destroyed hundreds of Rohingya villages and forced nearly 700,000 Rohingya to flee Myanmar for Bangladesh's Cox's Bazar district. During August 25 and September 24, 2017 at least 6700 Rohingya were killed (Doctors without Borders, 2017).

Since the re-eruption of conflict and violence against the Rohingya in 2012, some authors (Cheesman, 2017; Kipgen, 2013; Parnini, 2013; Siddiquee, 2020; Thawnghmung, 2016; Ware & Laoutides, 2018) have opined that the recent resurgence is the result of distrust and fear between the Rohingya Muslims and Myanmar Buddhists. Their animosity is based on four overarching factors: cultural differences, competition for land and resources, political mobilisation based on indigeneity by the Rakhine Nationalities Development Party (RNDP) and the National Democratic Party for Development (NDPD), and a political opening that created space for the expression of pent-up frustrations (Thawnghmung, 2016, p. 528). Moreover, ultranationalists such as Ma Ba Tha have gained widespread grassroots support in the name of protecting the Buddhist people and their religion. However, the violence has had a particular gendered and racialised quality that can be included in a broader framework of far right populism in the age of posttruth politics and fake news. In the posttruth era, populists/nationalists do not use objective facts in shaping public opinion; rather, they appeal to emotion and personal belief. Thus, it would help to unveil the constructed sexist and racist features of the current crisis and how, in far-right populist discourse and practices, Muslim minority citizens are affected by gendered anti-Muslim racism (Vieten, 2016).

ACTORS IN CONFLICT: THE ULTRANATIONALIST BUDDHISTS AND ARSA

With the end of military rule in 2011, Myanmar faced an enormous surge in ultra-Buddhist nationalists in the public sphere. Some of these well-known groups[2] include '969', Ma Ba Tha (Organisation for Protection of Race and Religion), Buddha Dhamma Parahita Foundation, Dhamma Wunthanu Rakhita, and various 'myo-chit'[3] youth groups. Their religious chauvinism is directed mainly against

Islam and Muslims. Some of their slogans, such as 'Burma for the Burmans' and 'To be Burman is to be Buddhist', represent their call to protect and promote Buddhism in Myanmar while excluding other religious minorities, such as Muslims, Hindus, and Christians. While sporadic mob violence and hate speech, particularly against the Muslim Rohingya, has been addressed in mainstream news, understanding the dynamics of the conflict requires a deeper scholarly understanding to better address the Rohingya crisis. This section explores the roles that two specific groups, '969' and the Ma Ba Tha movement, have played in the Rohingya crisis. They are not the only movements that have promoted and reinforced far right populist sentiments, but the narratives and practices they promote provide clear evidence of a racial and gendered focus towards the protection of Buddhist and Buddhist women from Muslim men.

The '969' movement is a nationwide popular Buddhist nationalist movement in Myanmar. As such, it intends to protect the Buddhist people and religion from Muslims. The name '969' is a numerological reference to the three Jewels of Buddhism, based on the Buddhist *dhamma* (teachings of the Buddha). The first '9' represents the nine noble attributes of Buddha, including *araham* (holy), *samma-sambuddho* (self-enlightened), *vijjacarana-sampanno* (proficient in knowledge and conduct), *sugato* (sublime), *lokavidu* (knows all worlds), *anuttaro-purisa-dhammasarathi* (peerless charioteer to tame men), *sattha-deva-manussanam* (teacher of Gods and men), *buddho* (knows the Truth) *and bhagava* (glorious) (Nyunt, 1981). The number '6' represents the attributes of the dhamma (teachings of the Buddha) and the last '9' represents the attributes of the Buddhist sangha (the community of monks and nuns). The visibility of the movement increased when its apparent leader, a Buddhist monk named Ashin Wirathu, was jailed in 2001 for his involvement in the group and for engaging in hate crimes. The movement received wider attention upon Wirathu's release from jail under the general amnesty for the political prisoner in 2012 (Thompson, 2013).

The Buddhist numerical reference was created to counter the Muslim numerical reference of '786' (Schonthal & Walton, 2016). In South Asian Muslim culture, 786 represents *Bismillah ar-Rahman ar-Rahim* ('in the name of Allah, the compassionate, the merciful'). Across South Asia, many business enterprises and shops hang this symbol in front of their shops and enterprises to mark them as Muslim, as a sign of blessing from Allah, and as a halal enterprise (Schonthal & Walton, 2016; van Klinken & Aung, 2017). It is evident from the Buddhist narratives, as one Buddhist woman relayed to the BBC, 'we use the sticker [of 969] to show our respect and love for Buddhism and to show that we are Buddhist'.[4] Therefore, Buddhist monks encouraged their people to use '969' to counteract their neighbouring Muslim business enterprises so that Burmese shoppers buy from Buddhist businesses, not Muslim. '969' was banned in 2014 because of its role in spreading hate speech and anti-Muslim propaganda. This did not curb the development of populist Buddhist sentiments, as the '969' bans contributed to the subsequent rise of Ma Ba Tha.

The Organisation for the Protection of Race and Religion, popularly known as Ma Ba Tha, originated in 2014 and was led by the recently released political prisoner, Wirathu, who was already widely known for his involvement in anti-Muslim propaganda, hate speech, and riots. Ma Ba Tha has run Sunday schools and other community events, including social welfare provisions, which have become popular across Myanmar. Their aim is to protect Buddhism and regain the old Buddhist kingdom from the seventh century, which included present-day Afghanistan, Pakistan, India, and Bangladesh. They blame Muslim conquerors for decimating the former glory of the Buddhist kingdom when they invaded the Buddhist kingdom and converted people into Islam. Ultranationalist Buddhists fear that the Rohingya will do the same to Myanmar. As a result, many monks consider Muslims to be an existential threat to Myanmar and Buddhism. The populist movements '969' and Ma Ba Tha have been using different social media outlets to spread fear and hatred against the Muslim Rohingya, employing threat narratives that are gendered and racialised. The State Sangha Maha Nayaka Committee—the country's highest official Buddhist authority that regulates Buddhist clergy—banned Ma Ba Tha on May 23, 2017 because of its alleged role in violence against the Muslim Rohingya and the spread of hate speech and other defamatory propaganda. However, Ma Ba Tha re-emerged with a different name, the 'Buddha Dhamma Parahita Foundation', which replicates the former's organisational structure and activities (Myanmar Times, 2017).

The situation in Myanmar is complex and does not consist solely of populist or nationalist movements dominated by one narrative. On the opposite side of the spectrum is the Rohingya ultranationalist organisation—the Arakan Rohingya Salvation Army (ARSA). ARSA is the only organisation representing the Rohingya that is fighting for the rights of

Rohingya Muslims within a nationalist and populist narrative. ARSA was created by a group of 20 people from the Rohingya diaspora in Saudi Arabia during 2013 or 2014 as a result of the violence between Buddhists and Muslims in Myanmar in 2012. Its aim is to promote and protect the rights of the Rohingya and to ensure their rights to full citizenship status. In one of its Twitter messages, ARSA claims that it 'only legitimately and objectively operates as an ethno-nationalist movement within its ancestral homeland (Arakan) in Burma'.[5] However, ultra-Buddhist nationalists, ordinary Burmese, and many news media outlets tend to consider it an Islamist militant organisation that is waging jihad. Thus, they claim that ARSA is a security threat not only to Buddhism but also to the country. However, Fair (2018) argues that 'while many in the "Islamist terrorism" industry have been quick to paint ARSA with the jihadi brush, I am skeptical of ARSA's Islamist bona fides. ARSA has assiduously rejected Islamist appeals'. Moreover, ARSA does not possess modern weapons to carry out massive and large-scale attacks; in their previous attacks on Myanmar police posts, they used bamboo sticks and homemade bombs. The Myanmar government has banned this militant organisation.

There is a widespread belief by the Myanmar authorities and the Buddhist population generally that the general Rohingya population is actively participating in ARSA and its arms struggle. This assumption was not borne out during the interviews conducted for this book. Likewise, Amnesty International believes that ARSA mobilises many, but not all, Rohingya villagers. Of my Rohingya interviewees, only two of the respondents said that they had heard anything about ARSA, but they did not know who actually engaged in fighting against the Buddhist Burmese. One of the informants, who is also one of the Majhis[6] in the Rohingya camp, told me that the Buddhist Rakhine believe that all Rohingya youth belong to ARSA (Interview: 2018MRMM1). When I asked him about ARSA's attacks on the military check posts in recent years, he claimed these all are fake news. He said, 'we could not even keep a *dao* (a traditional weapon for chopping) at home without their [the authorities'] permission; how could ARSA have a weapon to attack the Magh[7]'?

This respondent contradicted ARSA's self-portrait as an armed militant group in its official Twitter site[8] and in its official publication from 2019 entitled 'Reviving the Courageous Heart: A Report by Arakan Rohingya Salvation Army'.[9] However, ARSA was evidently armed when it attacked a Hindu community in Rakhine state in August 2017. As Amnesty International claims, ARSA 'is responsible for at least one, and potentially a second, massacre of up to 99 Hindu women, men, and children as well as additional unlawful killings and abductions of Hindu villagers' (Amnesty International, 2018). Moreover, ARSA was also responsible for forcefully converting Hindu women to Islam and later marrying them. During my interview with a Hindu Rohingya man living in the Rohingya camps, he told me, 'We are more fearful of ARSA than the Burmese military'. When I asked why, he replied, 'We fled to Bangladesh to escape from the torture from ARSA' (Interview: 2018HRM2).

THE STATE, THE MILITARY AND THE MONKS: A COMPLEX INTERPLAY

To understand the Rohingya crisis, it is important to unpack the complex relationship between the state, the military, and the monks. Although Myanmar has returned to democracy after a long period of authoritarian rule, it is nevertheless backed by the military and thus could be called a 'quasidemocracy'. At first glance, it might not be entirely clear how Buddhist monks are involved in this scenario, but there are several examples of their interrelatedness. For example, in a gathering of thousands of people in Yangon, the radical monk Ashin Wirathu praised the military establishment for its role in the Rohingya genocide. In one rally, he claimed that military-linked lawmakers deserved to be glorified like Buddha and that 'only the military … protects both our country and our religion', while in another rally in October 2018, he condemned the decision by the International Criminal Court (ICC) to pursue a case against Myanmar's military for its persecution of the Rohingya (Beech, 2019).

The monks and the military have not always had a comfortable relationship and, indeed, when examining the history of military rule in Myanmar since 1948, the relationship has been highly contentious. For example, many monks were arrested and detained for their involvement in the 'Saffron revolution' of 2007. The Saffron revolution was led by the monks to protest against the military dictatorship and the consequent political and economic crisis (i.e., price hikes). The revolution ended due to the military junta's crackdown on the protesters. However, this relationship changed with the advent of democratic governance. The opening of Myanmar in 2011 and its transition to democracy fostered a new alliance between the monks, the military, and the state based on a Buddhist nationalist narrative. The then-president, Thein Sein, openly supported ultranationalist monks. He declared Wirathu to be a son of Lord Buddha who is spreading a message of peace and love. When, in 2013, *Time* magazine called Ashin Wirathu 'The face of Buddhist terror' and the 'Buddhist Bin Laden',[10] President Thein Sien gave a statement in his official website that claimed the *Time* magazine report had 'undermined efforts to rebuild trust between faiths and that the monk's order was striving for peace and prosperity'. Thien Sien further claimed that magazine article's characterisation of Buddhists would create 'a misunderstanding of Buddhism, which has existed for thousands of years and is the religion of the majority of our citizens' (BBC, 2013, para 3&5).

Wirathu, who has been instrumental in leading the Buddhist nationalist movements either through '969' or through Ma Ba Tha, has powerful connections with the top level of the military. He has had strong support from San Sint, a former lieutenant general in the military regime and the Minister of Religious Affairs for the Union Solidarity and Development Party (USDP), who has vowed 969's propagation as messages of peace (Routray, 2014). Wirathu's connections include other significant military leaders, for example, General Ne Win (Head of State, 1962–1981) and Than Shwe (the junta leader during 1992–2011), who was responsible for the murder of hundreds of monks during the Saffron Revolution (Coclanis, 2013). These are military actors who had a role in the previous authoritarian rule and have continued under the democracy that was forged in 2011. This mix of actors—the state, the military, and ultranationalist monks—reached a consensus over the Burmese identity to determine who should and should not belong to the Burmese polity. Wade (2017) explained how the contestation over an ethnic minority's identity was jointly manipulated by Buddhist extremists and the oppressive military government in Myanmar to construct the Rohingya as 'others' who were, consequently, a threat to Buddhism and Myanmar. This allowed them to justify the forcible removal of Rohingya from the Rakhine State.

These three groups of actors have actively used various tactics to popularise anti-Muslim and pro-Buddhist propaganda among the general population, using different social media such as Facebook, Twitter, and YouTube. Facebook, in particular, played a distinct role in igniting the conflict. As Milmo (2021, para 8) mentioned, 'Facebook admitted in 2018 that it had not done enough to prevent the incitement of violence and hate speech against the Rohingya, the Muslim minority in Myanmar … "Facebook has become a means for those seeking to spread hate and cause harm, and posts have been linked to offline violence"'.

Conclusion

The protracted Rohingya crisis is characterised by intricate dynamics surrounding self-identity (as Rohingya) and ascribed identity (as illegal Bengali), and the consequent denial of citizenship for the Rohingya. This denial created conflict, tension, and violence that resulted in the forced displacement of many Rohingya from Myanmar. The Rohingya became victims of arbitrary violence, such as the burning of houses and properties. The main perpetrators of the violence were the military and ultranationalist Buddhist entities of Myanmar. The Buddhist monks, previous enemies of the military establishment due to Saffron Revolution of 2007, become allies against a common enemy, the Rohingya. Ordinary Rohingya civilians were the main victims of such violence. From the Rohingya side, a militant Rohingya organisation named ARSA was also involved in violence through attacking Myanmar security forces bases. However, the trajectory of recent violence against the Rohingya has been predominantly unidirectional, with eruptions commencing in 2012 and resurging in subsequent years until reaching a climax in 2017. Since August 25, 2017, more than 700,000 Rohingya have fled Myanmar in a bid to preserve their lives, seeking refuge in Bangladesh. Between 2012 and 2017, the predominant manifestations of violence included various forms of direct violence, such as murder, killings, mob violence, and sexual violence, including instances of rape. The Rohingya community has also been subjected to structural violence, encompassing discrimination, pervasive poverty, constrained access to resources, limitations on property rights, educational constraints, and restricted mobility. However, the historical backdrop of antagonism has deep roots, tracing back to the British mobilisation of labour in Myanmar during their rule from 1885 to 1948. The issue became particularly acute following Myanmar's independence in 1948. Over the years, multifaceted processes have contributed to the predicament of the Rohingya. In the chapter that follows, I focus on the multidimensional vulnerabilities and violence against the Rohingya over the years, particularly during the period 2012–2017, with a focus on the gendered nature of the violence.

Notes

1. See detail about ARSA's different posts and claims at https://twitter.com/ARSA_Official
2. For a detail discussion on Ma Ba Tha see, International Crisis Group, 'Buddhism and State Power in Myanmar', *Asia Report no.290*, Brussels: ICG, 5 Sept. 2017).
3. Meaning 'nationalist', or literally 'love for one's own race'.
4. See https://www.youtube.com/watch?v=nSihfWY41So
5. See https://twitter.com/ARSA_Official/status/1149990453355225088
6. A majhi is a Rohingya leader who is in charge of a block in the Rohingya camps. It is part of the 'Majhi System' introduced by the Bangladeshi government for better governance of the Rohingya refugees.
7. *Magh* are the Arakanese people from Myanmar and in Bangladesh the Arakanese used be called *Magh* pirates. They were involved in plundering along the coast of Chittagong and in the rivers of Bengal. They also captured many Bengalis and sold them in the slave markets run by the Dutch East India Company in the seventeenth century.
8. See the ARSA official Twitter site, https://twitter.com/arsa_official?lang=en
9. See the video made by ARSA entitled 'Reviving the Courageous Hearts' at https://issuu.com/arsapublisher/docs/report_1_final_2, access on 07.07.2020
10. See the *Time* magazine vol. 182, no. 1 that made a front-cover page entitled 'The Face of Buddhist Terror', 1 July 2013.

References

AFP. (2017). *Mass grave of 28 Hindus found in Myanmar: Army*. https://www.afp.com/en/news/23/mass-grave-28-hindus-found-myanmar-army, accessed on December 17, 2019.

Akins, H. (2018). The Two Faces of Democratization in Myanmar: A Case Study of the Rohingya and Burmese Nationalism. *Journal of Muslim Minority Affairs, 38*(2), 229–245. https://doi.org/10.1080/13602004.2018.1475619

Alam, J. (2019). The Current Rohingya Crisis in Myanmar in Historical Perspective. *Journal of Muslim Minority Affairs, 39*(1), 1–25. https://doi.org/10.1080/13602004.2019.1575560

Albert, E., & Maizland, L. (2020). *The Rohingya Crisis*. C. o. F. Relations. https://www.cfr.org/backgrounder/rohingya-crisis#chapter-title-0-1, accessed on January 24, 2020.

Aljazeera. (2017). *Deadly clashes erupt in Myanmar's restive Rakhine state*. https://www.aljazeera.com/news/2017/8/26/deadly-clashes-erupt-in-myanmars-restive-rakhine-state, accessed on December 17, 2019.

Amnesty International. (2018). *Myanmar: New Evidence Reveals Rohingya Armed Group Massacred Scores in Rakhine State.* https://www.amnesty.org/en/latest/news/2018/05/myanmar-new-evidence-reveals-rohingya-armed-group-massacred-scores-in-rakhine-state/, accessed on June 27, 2019.

ASEAN Economist. (2017). *Rohingya 'Insurgent' Camp Raided.* A. Economist. https://www.aseaneconomist.com/rohingya-insurgent-camp-raided, accessed on January 29, 2020.

BBC. (2013, June 24). Burmese Leader Defends 'Anti Muslim' Monk Ashin Wirathu. *BBC.* https://www.bbc.com/news/world-asia-23027492, accessed on January 28, 2020.

BBC. (2016a). Myanmar policemen killed in Rakhine border attack. *BBC News.* https://web.archive.org/web/20161011223358/http://www.bbc.com/news/world-asia-37601928, accessed April 29, 2020.

BBC. (2016b). Rakhine unrest leaves four Myanmar soldiers dead. *BBC News.* https://www.bbc.com/news/world-asia-37627498, access April 29, 2020.

Beech, H. (2019, December 9). Buddhists Go To Battle: When Nationalism Overrides Pacifism. *The New York Times.* https://www.nytimes.com/2019/07/08/world/asia/buddhism-militant-rise.html, accessed on March 28, 2020.

Berlie, J. A. (2008). *The Burmanization of Myanmar's Muslims.* White Lotus Press.

Buchanan, F. (1799). *Asiatic Researches, 5,* 219–240. (Calcutta Edition) (London). https://books.google.no/books?hl=en&lr=&id=cxNnAAAAcAAJ&oi=fnd&pg=PA219&ots=V0U42gEeq6&sig=BqrlboI3ncyn_ovdEaqQVoUFH-A&redir_esc=y#v=onepage&q&f=true

Cheesman, N. (2017). How in Myanmar 'National Races' Came to Surpass Citizenship and Exclude Rohingya. *Journal of Contemporary Asia, 47*(3), 461–483. https://doi.org/10.1080/00472336.2017.1297476

Coclanis, P. A. (2013). Terror in Burma: Buddhists vs. Muslims. *World Affairs, 176*(4), 25–33. http://www.jstor.org/stable/43554876

Doctors without Borders. (2017). *MSF Surveys Estimate That at Least 6,700 Rohingya Were Killed During the Attacks in Myanmar.* https://www.msf.org/myanmarbangladesh-msf-surveys-estimate-least-6700-rohingya-were-killed-during-attacks-myanmar, accessed on February 13, 2019.

Fair, C. C. (2018, December 9). Arakan Rohingya Salvation Army: Not the Jihadis You Might Expect. *Lawfare.* https://www.lawfareblog.com/arakan-rohingya-salvation-army-not-jihadis-you-might-expect, accessed on January 27, 2020.

Gittleman, A., Brodney, M., & Atkinson, H. G. (2013). *Patterns of Anti-Muslim Violence in Burma: A Call for Accountability and Prevention.* P. f. H. Rights. chrome-extension://efaidnbmnnnibpcajpcglclefindmkaj/https://academic-works.cuny.edu/cgi/viewcontent.cgi?referer=&httpsredir=1&article=1462&context=cc_pubs, accessed on March 21, 2021.

Head, J. (2017). *Rohingya Crisis: Finding out the Truth About Arsa Militants.* BBC News, BBC.

Human Rights Watch. (2013). *'All You Can Do Is Pray': Crimes Against Humanity and Ethnic Cleansing of Rohingya Muslims in Burma's Arakan State* (ISBN: 978-1-62313-0053). H. R. Watch.

International Crisis Group. (2012). *Myanmar Conflict Alert: Preventing Communal Bloodshed and Building Better Relations.* I. C. Group. https://www.crisisgroup.org/asia/south-east-asia/myanmar/myanmar-conflict-alert-preventing-communal-bloodshed-and-building-better-relations, accessed on May 5, 2019.

Kipgen, N. (2013). Conflict in Rakhine State in Myanmar: Rohingya Muslims' Conundrum. *Journal of Muslim Minority Affairs, 33*(2), 298–310. https://doi.org/10.1080/13602004.2013.810117

Kyaw, N. N. (2019). Adulteration of Pure Native Blood by Aliens? Mixed Race Kapya in Colonial and Post-Colonial Myanmar. *Social Identities, 25*(3), 345–359. https://doi.org/10.1080/13504630.2018.1499223

McCarthy, G., & Menager, J. (2017). Gendered Rumours and the Muslim Scapegoat in Myanmar's Transition. *Journal of Contemporary Asia, 47*(3), 396–412. https://doi.org/10.1080/00472336.2017.1304563

Médecins Sans Frontières. (2002, March). *10 Years for the Rohingya Refugees in Bangladesh: Past, Present and Future.* pp. 1–45. M. S. Frontieres-Holland https://www.msf.fr/sites/www.msf.fr/files/2002-03-01-Wiggers.pdf, accessed on September 28, 2018.

Milmo, D. (2021, December 6). Rohingya Sue Facebook for £150bn Over Myanmar genocide. *The Guardian.* https://www.theguardian.com/technology/2021/dec/06/rohingya-sue-facebook-myanmar-genocide-us-uk-legal-action-social-media-violence, accessed March 21, 2024.

Myanmar Times. (2017, May 29). *Ma-Ba-Tha to Continue Under New Name.* https://www.mmtimes.com/national-news/yangon/26171-ma-ba-tha-to-continue-under-new-name.html, accessed on May 25, 2020.

Nyunt, A. T. (1981). *The Nine Supreme Attributes of the Lord Buddha.* http://www.myanmarnet.net/nibbana/buddha9.htm, accessed on August 21, 2019.

Parashar, A., & Alam, J. (2019). The National Laws of Myanmar: Making of Statelessness for the Rohingya. *International Migration, 57*(1), 94–108. https://doi.org/10.1111/imig.12532

Parnini, S. N. (2013). The Crisis of the Rohingya as a Muslim Minority in Myanmar and Bilateral Relations with Bangladesh. *Journal of Muslim Minority Affairs, 33*(2), 281–297. https://doi.org/10.1080/13602004.2013.826453

Qnungo, S. B. D. (1988). *A History of Chittagong (From Ancient Times Down to 1761)* (Vol. 1). Dipankar Qanungo.

Republic of the Union of Myanmar. (2013). *Final Report of Inquiry Commission on Sectarian Violence in Rakhine State.* https://www.burmalibrary.org/docs15/Rakhine_Commission_Report-en-red.pdf, accessed on June 17, 2020.

Routray, B. P. (2014). *Profiling the 969 Movement' in Myanmar in Transition: Ethnic Conflicts, External Interests and Ethnic Conflicts, External Interests and Political Changes Political Changes*. IPCS.

Schonthal, B., & Walton, M. J. (2016). The (New) Buddhist Nationalisms? Symmetries and Specificities in Sri Lanka and Myanmar. *Contemporary Buddhism, 17*(1), 81–115. https://doi.org/10.1080/14639947.2016.1162419

Siddiquee, M. A. (2020). The Portrayal of the Rohingya Genocide and Refugee Crisis in the Age of Post-Truth Politics. *Asian Journal of Comparative Politics, 5*(2), 89–103. https://doi.org/10.1177/2057891119864454

Slodkowski, A. (2016, November 15). Myanmar Army Says 86 Killed in Fighting in Northwest. *Reuters.* https://in.reuters.com/article/myanmar-rohingya-idINKBN13A11N, accessed on October 27, 2017.

Thawnghmung, A. M. (2016). The Politics of Indigeneity in Myanmar: Competing Narratives in Rakhine State. *Asian Ethnicity, 17*(4), 527–547. https://doi.org/10.1080/14631369.2016.1179096

The Economist. (2012). Unforgiving History: Why Buddhists and Muslims in Rakhine State in Myanmar Are at Each Others' Throats. *Banyan.* https://www.economist.com/news/asia/21565638-why-buddhists-and-muslims-rakhine-state-myanmar-are-each-others%E2%80%99-throats-unforgiving, accessed on July 3, 2023.

Thompson, N. G. (2013). *The 969 Movement and Burmese Anti-Muslim Nationalism in Context'.* Retrieved March 19, 2019, from http://www.buddhistpeacefellowship.org/the-969-movement-and-burmese-anti-muslim-nationalism-in-context/, accessed on March 19, 2019.

UNHCR. (2013). *One Year On: Displacement in Rakhine State, Myanmar.* UNHCR. https://www.unhcr.org/en-ie/news/briefing/2013/6/51b1af0b6/year-displacement-rakhine-state-myanmar.html, accessed on January 21, 2019.

van Klinken, G., & Aung, S. M. T. (2017). The Contentious Politics of Anti-Muslim Scapegoating in Myanmar. *Journal of Contemporary Asia, 47*(3), 353–375. https://doi.org/10.1080/00472336.2017.1293133

Van Schendel, W. (Ed.). (1992). *Francis Buchanan in South East Bengal (1798): His Journey to Chittagong, The Chittagong Hill Tracts, Noakhali and Comilla.* University Press Limited.

Vieten, U. M. (2016). Far Right Populism and Women: The Normalisation of Gendered Anti-Muslim Racism and Gendered Culturalism in The Netherlands. *Journal of Intercultural Studies, 37*(6), 621–636. https://doi.org/10.1080/07256868.2016.1235024

Wade, F. (2017). *Myanmar's Enemy Within: Buddhist Violence and the Making of a Muslim 'Other'.* Zed Books.

Ware, A., & Laoutides, C. (2018). *Myanmar's 'Rohingya' Conflict.* Hurst Publishers.

Open Access This chapter is licensed under the terms of the Creative Commons Attribution 4.0 International License (http://creativecommons.org/licenses/by/4.0/), which permits use, sharing, adaptation, distribution and reproduction in any medium or format, as long as you give appropriate credit to the original author(s) and the source, provide a link to the Creative Commons license and indicate if changes were made.

The images or other third party material in this chapter are included in the chapter's Creative Commons license, unless indicated otherwise in a credit line to the material. If material is not included in the chapter's Creative Commons license and your intended use is not permitted by statutory regulation or exceeds the permitted use, you will need to obtain permission directly from the copyright holder.

CHAPTER 4

Gendered and Racialised Vulnerabilities and Violence Against the Rohingya in Myanmar

Abstract This chapter presents gender differentiated forms of direct, structural, cultural and symbolic violence experienced by the Rohingya while they were in Myanmar. The documented atrocities, committed mainly by the Myanmar military, have placed the Rohingya in a state of ongoing discrimination and oppression. Within Myanmar, Rohingya women face a dual burden: enduring physical violence and mental anguish from military and societal forces, compounded by the patriarchal structure within their own community. Structural violence, such as educational discrimination, pervasive poverty, and lack of access to social and community life have affected Rohingya women, men, and children differently. A gendered narrative of threat portrays Rohingya women as ugly and reproductive dangers to Buddhism, while Rohingya men are framed as threats to nationalism and Buddhism. These religious and cultural narratives have served to justify 'othering' and various forms of violence by the Myanmar military.

Keywords Everyday racism • Gendered rumours • Othering • Sexual violence • Gendered mobility • Intermarriage • Motherhood

© The Author(s) 2024   45
M. M. Salehin, *Gendered Vulnerabilities and Violence in Forced Migration*, https://doi.org/10.1007/978-3-031-62435-3_4

INTRODUCTION

Rohingya women, men, and children in Myanmar endured various forms of violence, encompassing direct, structural, and cultural dimensions, as well as confronting multidimensional vulnerabilities both prior to and during the mass exodus in 2017. A comprehensive understanding of the Rohingya crisis necessitates an exploration of the underlying gendered nature and narratives inherent in the violence, considering its intersectional dimensions. This chapter explores the intersectional dimensions of the crisis in the Rakhine State and next chapter will delve into the experiences of the Rohingya refugees upon reaching what is ostensibly considered a safe destination, Bangladesh. This discussion explicates why the Rohingya people in general, and men in particular, have been relegated to the status of a 'monstrous other' that threatens the existence of Buddhism and Burmeseness. It also examines how cultural logic serves to justify the claim of Burmese superiority over the Rohingya, characterising them as the 'ignorant Bengali *Kala*'. Additionally, the discussion includes an analysis of gendered rumours, instances of sexual violence directed at both Rohingya men and women, the dynamics and politics of intermarriage, reproduction, and motherhood and the interplay of ultra-Buddhist nationalism and Buddhist women in Myanmar.

'MONSTROUS OTHER', ROHINGYA MEN, AND THE EXISTENTIAL THREAT TO BUDDHISM

Before their mass exodus, the Rohingya people in general, and men in particular, were portrayed as the 'monstrous other' on various social media platforms, including Facebook and Twitter, as well as in public sermons. This construction of the 'threat image' of the Rohingya is gendered in nature. Rohingya femininity, reproductive capacity, and motherhood became associated with the 'dangerous breeder' of the Muslim population and consequent threats to Buddhism. Men, on the other hand, came to be portrayed as potential kidnappers, perpetrators of forced marriage and forced conversion of Buddhist women to Islam, and the ultimate threat to Buddhism and Burmese nationalism. The main perpetrators of these portrayals were the Buddhist monks, the military, and their allies. Although creating the Rohingya as an 'other' was in the making for a long time, with the rise and increased use of social media—and in particular with the uninterrupted flow of mis/disinformation—the Rohingya became a 'radical other' or a 'monstrous other', a source of horror and terror (Croft, 2012). Since Myanmar's transition to democracy, there has been a rapid proliferation of Facebook usage. Internet access in Myanmar has largely been synonymous with Facebook. On Facebook and offline, ultranationalists have framed Muslims as posing both a personal threat and a threat to the Buddhist majority nation. As Fink (2018) argues, 'Facebook posts and messages have played a key part in spreading fear and inciting anti-Muslim violence in Myanmar' (Fink, 2018, p. 49).

The nature of such social media posts demonises the Muslim Rohingya, calling them 'violent extremists' and 'terrorists' who practise 'violent Islam'. The statements made by different actors including government officials, politicians, religious authorities, and military commanders, alongside those of the direct perpetrators, unveiled a vision founded on exclusionary principles, manifesting through the deployment of linguistic expression and corresponding actions. An illustration of this can be observed in the utilisation of phrases such as 'go away', 'you do not belong here', 'you are Bengali', and 'we will kill you all' by the perpetrators, directed towards the Rohingya Muslim population, which serves to reinforce the aforementioned assertion (Office of the United Nations High Commissioner for Human Rights, 2019). According to Democracy Reporting International (DRI),[1] one of the Buddhist Facebook groups called 'Platform for Ma Ba Tha Supporters' posted approximately 14,720 posts from June 2016 to November 2017, which received 1,922,891 likes, 193,195 comments, and 470,820 shares. Before Facebook removed his account, Ashin Wirathu,[2] a Buddhist monk, had 4916 Friends and 37,862 Followers (BBC, 2018). Wirathu was already widely known for waging anti-Muslim propaganda, dissemination of hate speech, and instigation of riots. He led the ultranationalist organisation known as Ma Ba Tha (the Organisation for the Protection of Race and Religion). Wirathu posted anti-Muslim statements regularly on Facebook, such as 'You can be full of kindness and love, but you cannot sleep next to a mad dog [the Muslim] ... I call them troublemakers because they are troublemakers ... If we are weak, our land will become Muslim'. He proudly claimed in his sermon, 'I am proud to be called a radical Buddhist' (Fuller, 2013, para 3). Facebook was also used extensively by military and state personnel. For example, Zaw Htay, a spokesman for the country's de facto leader, Daw Aung San Suu Kyi, has shared dozens of posts on his Facebook page and Twitter account that include images said to show Rohingya burning their own homes. On August 18, 2018, Facebook removed 425 Facebook Pages, 17 Facebook Groups, 135 Facebook accounts and 15 Instagram accounts in Myanmar for engaging in coordinated inauthentic behavior on Facebook … Approximately 2.5 million people followed at least one of these Facebook Pages. Approximately 6400 people belonged to at least one of these Facebook Groups. Approximately 1300 people followed at least one of these Instagram accounts. (Meta, 2018, para 1)

Although Wirathu was eventually banned from Facebook, his different sermons remained available on YouTube, DVDs, booklets, as well as to thousands of students via their Sunday school. Filled with hate for Muslims, they portrayed Muslim Rohingya as dangerous and poisonous. For example, in one of his sermons, Wirathu says, 'They [Rohingya] target women every day and rape them'. However, during three phases of interviews with the Rohingya, only two respondents said they knew someone who married a Buddhist woman, and all the respondents opposed the Buddhist claim regarding the forced conversion and marrying of Buddhist women. In the words of one interviewee,

I haven't heard of anyone forcefully marrying any Buddhist girl. However, I came to know about a few Rohingya boys who used to study together with the Buddhist girls from their neighbourhood, and they fell in love with each other. Then, they wanted to marry each other. However, it was not legal in Myanmar, and if you do so, you will be in jail … Then, these two lovers either flee to Bangladesh or hide in the quiet mountains and marry each other. (Interview: 2022MRF3)

In another of his sermons, Wirathu said, 'Starting from today, do we need to protect our religion or not? People attending his sermon replied, 'Yes, your Reverence'. He then said, 'Snakes are poisonous wherever they are. You can't underestimate a snake just because there's only one. It's dangerous wherever it is. Muslims are just like that'. He justified his statement by adding, 'They will ask for an Islamic state and I worry they will set up a Muslim country. That with their population they will apply pressure by intermarrying our women' (SBS, 2013). In yet another sermons, Wirathu called for a boycott of all Muslim-owned businesses in order to weaken Muslims economically, arguing:

If you buy a good from a Muslim shop, your money just does not stop there … money will eventually be used against you to destroy your race and religion. That money will be used to get a Buddhist-Burmese woman and she will very soon be coerced or even forced to convert to Islam … once

[Muslims] become overly populous, they will overwhelm us and take over our country and make it an evil Islamic nation. (Bookbinder, 2013)

However, it was mainly the ultra-Buddhist monks and the military who waged a hate speech war against the Rohingya. All of my respondents told me that their relationship with the majority Buddhist Rakhine in Rakhine State was 'normal' until 2012. For example, one respondent told me,

> In Rakhine, we were the majority of Rohingyas and Magh [Arakan Buddhist]. We knew each other and had regular communication with each other. When we went to the shops or markets, the Maghs and Rohingyas went to the same shop together. We felt like we were relatives. However, since 2012, the picture has changed! Until 2012, during the *Eid Qurban* [the second largest religious festival for Muslims], many Maghs – adults and children both – used to visit us and enjoy and then leave. We used to do the same. We used to go to their houses on various occasions, we used to attend their *dawat* [invitation]. We used to mix with them and play *Pani Khela* [Water Festival]. I used to do many such things with them. (Interview: 2022MRM3)

It is also important to mention that the social media representations, rumours, and propaganda perpetuated by Wirathu and other ultranationalists have a gender dimension. There are claims to the 'collective ownership' of their (Buddhist) women and that the men must take on the role of 'protector' of the nation-sate and the women (McCarthy & Menager, 2017). They were to protect their women from the Bengali *kala*.

Bengali *Kala*: From Everyday Racism to Political Rhetoric in Myanmar

Kala or *Kula* is a derogatory term used by the Burmese against the Rohingya. Use of this term dates back to historical Indian communities living in Myanmar. Today's understanding of '*Kala*' or '*Kula*' is far more restrictive and derogatory than its eighteenth century meaning and serves as a source of structural violence. In the Burmese language, *Kala* or *Kula* applies to any 'foreigner' coming to Myanmar from outside. Here, etymologically, '*Ku-la*' comprises '*ku*', which refers to crossing a maritime space (mainly the Bay of Bengal), and '*la*', meaning 'to come'. *Kala*, in Bengali, Hindi, and other languages derived from Sanskrit, means 'black' and thus refers to the dark-skinned (mainly Indian) non-Buddhists living in Myanmar. However, in ancient Pali, *kala* meant 'noble'. Since the nineteenth century mass mobilisation of Indian communities by the British Empire in Burma, the current derogatory connotation of *kala* has become increasingly prevalent in popular Burmese culture. Over time, anti-*kala* rhetoric has been used for Indophobic political ends by the Burmese. Finally, '*kala*' has become a symbol of Islamophobia, mainly against Indian Muslims and, more exclusively, against the Rohingya (Egreteau, 2011).

All the Rohingya respondents told me that they had been labelled 'Bengali *Kala*' by their Rakhine counterparts, including neighbours, schoolteachers, monks, and the military. I then asked my respondents what people mean when they call a Rohingya person a 'Bengali *Kala*'. According to one respondent, it meant 'illiterate'. Another respondent mentioned that it is now used exclusively towards Muslim Rohingya. For him, it is an expression of Islamophobia; he told me,

> They used to abuse us by calling us *kala* and torture us just because we are Muslims. We do not follow Buddhism, Christianity or Hinduism. We had some Hindu boys with us in our class who did not follow Islam, so they were not tortured or abused as *kala*. It is clearly used to separate the Muslim as ignorant and different (*forok*) from the whole society. (Interview: 2022MRM1)

This statement resonates with the claim by Egreteau (2011, p. 50) that, 'Burmese Indian communities of Hindu, Sikh and Christian background are today facing far less violent and open hostility from the rest of the Burmese society, compared to years and decades ago'. This can even be traced back to the 1930s, as Bowser (2021, p. 1140) argued: 'Hindu nationalists were successful in convincing Burmese fascists that they were brethren in their mutual struggle against Islam and its supposed attempts to divide communities'.

Calling the Rohingya 'Bengali *kala*' has a traumatic impact on them. One of my respondents told me how she feels and what *kala* truly means to her:

> They used to call us *kala*, which basically meant they hated us. *Kala* is equivalent to having no education, being Bengali, and having no knowledge (*elom nai*). Those who do not understand what is good and what is bad are *kala*. We are beasts, meaning the original meaning of the word *kala* is beast. Just as beasts do not know the difference between good and bad, they call

us *kala* as they thought we were the beasts ... We had no value to them. They could do whatever they wanted ... in Bangladesh when there is a program (for example, an annual school function or any public social event), there is no caste judgment in the program, everyone can go, whoever wants to attend. However, we who were Muslims could not attend the school program which was an annual event in Burma. We could not go. Our friend who studied in the same class could attend the program, but we never got that kind of opportunity in our life. If we compare our childhood and school life with the way we were able to live in Bangladesh, we feel very insignificant. Why are we such an insignificant nation (*niso koum/zati*) in the world? Always this question comes to my mind! (Interview: 2022MRF4)

GENDERED RUMOURS, ROHINGYA WOMEN, THE MILITARY, AND THE ULTRA-BUDDHIST NATIONALISTS

In an earlier study addressing the gendered dimension of rumour in riots in the US, Marilyn Johnson explains how gendered ideologies sparked the riot. In the rumour narratives during the US riots, women appeared either as victims of rape or as tortured mothers. Men appeared either as lusty rapists or as noble protectors. As gender and racial ideologies are intimately linked, the deployment of the above images helped forge a defensive collective identity. This, in turn, facilitated the outbreak of violence (Johnson, 1998).

Analysing different media sources and listening to the Rohingya respondents in Bangladesh, I found the same gendered rumour narratives and logic that sparked, sustained, and justified the cultural violence against the Muslim Rohingya in Myanmar. Both the 2012 riot in Rakhine State and the 2014 riot between the Muslim Rohingya and the Buddhist Burmese in Mandalay started with a rumour of a Buddhist woman being raped by Muslim men. As soon as the news of this rape was broadcast in state media, it went viral via different social media platforms. Viral mages of the victims helped to ignite the riot.

In regions characterised by political instability and conflict, rumours have served to instigate and intensify various forms of violence, such as riots, ethnic conflicts, and genocide. This phenomenon, which has been observed across diverse historical contexts and geographical locations worldwide, also exhibits a gendered nature. For instance, Gallimore (2008) demonstrates that, in the case of the 1994 Rwandan genocide, gendered linguistic and historical norms were rewritten and perpetuated as crucial tropes supporting the genocide and the widespread perpetration of sexual violence that targeted Tutsi women (Gallimore, 2008). An extremist magazine called *Kangura* promoted the 'Hutu Ten Commandments', which outlined guidelines for ethnic segregation and prohibited mixed marriages between Hutu men and Tutsi women. Anyone who violated these guidelines by marrying, befriending, or employing a Tutsi woman was labelled a traitor (Okech, 2021).

However, in the era of social media, the proliferation of fake news and disinformation has become pervasive. One consequence has been numerous instances of gendered rumours and associated violence. Farkhunda Malikzada's case stands as an example. On March 19, 2015, she was publicly lynched by a mob in Kabul, Afghanistan, amidst rumours claiming that she had burned the Quran. Following her murder, multiple versions of rumours spread throughout the country, each presenting differing explanations for her alleged actions. These rumours attained their intended effects by generating meaning as both a sense-making tool and a deliberate framing strategy employed by political groups and state officials (Ibrahimi, 2022).

In the Burmese narratives, Muslim men and the Rohingya are constructed as a 'threat', a 'poisonous snake', and a 'rapist'. In their social media propaganda, Buddhist monks have successfully created an image of Rohingya Muslims as 'fearsome others'. Rumours of rape and the forced conversion of Buddhist women to Islam have instigated Buddhist men, and the monks in particular, to assume the role of the 'protector' of Buddhist women (McCarthy & Menager, 2017). This is in line with what Veena Das calls 'gendered belonging to the nation-state', which explains how the nation-state normalises violence against the 'dangerous aliens' (Das, 2008). Using a metaphor of 'sex, death and reproduction', Das explains how and why the nation-state constructs man as a protector who 'should be ready to bear arms for the nation and be ready to die for it'. Women's reproduction is seen as rightly belonging to the state and the women's role is to 'bear "legitimate" children who will be, in turn, ready to die for the nation' (Das, 2008, p. 285). Contrary to the prevailing image of Buddhist women by the nation and the state, Rohingya women have been constructed as an ugly creature and thus prove an intimate link between race and gender. This is evident in the statements by the Myanmar military. For example, when asked about the soldier's role in sexual violence, Colonel Phone Tint, a minister for border security in the country's northern districts, replied, 'Look at those women [Rohingya] who are making these claims—would anyone want to rape them?' (Head, 2017, para 17). However, it has been widely claimed by different media and news sources, as well as the women I interviewed, that many women and girls were raped by the Magh (a term for Rakhine Buddhists in general). As one of my respondents reacted to the abovementioned claim,

> No ... no ... no ... it is totally wrong. I saw with my own eyes. During the year I was sitting for the matric exam [the school final exam], that time there was a girl named Rabiya in my neighbourhood. That girl was very beautiful, and she was 14 years old. The girl's house was next to the military base. During the day, the soldiers saw the girl, then at night they went to the girl's house. The soldiers tied girl's parents' mouths and tied them inside the house. They were six to seven people. They bit her throughout the whole body and raped her. Afterwards, they left the girl in a nearby canal. Looking at the girl's body, it appeared to be many dogs had bitten the girl. I know about another girl's incident. The girl was very beautiful, too. I don't agree Rohingya girls are not beautiful. What is most important to mention is that even old women were not spared from soldiers' hands, not to mention young girls. If they were girls, they started the torture. There are many such cases of inhumane torture, rape and killing. (Interview: 2022MRF5)

ROHINGYA WOMEN, VULNERABILITIES, AND SEXUAL VIOLENCE

Sexual violence and rape have been used as weapons of war and genocide. Some of the women I interviewed were the victims, or knew a family member and/or friends who were victims, of sexual violence by the Myanmar military. During my interviews with the Rohingya refugees in the Kutopalong camp, all the respondents claimed that they were physically and/or mentally tortured by the Magh, forcing them to flee to Bangladesh. One of them said,

> I had a cousin. She got married in our neighbouring village. One day, the whole village was set on fire by the military. Many people were killed. In addition, my sister who was married in that village, the day she came out of the village after the fire, she, her husband, and their children were attacked. Luckily, her husband managed to survive by hiding in the water. However, his wife and children were killed! My sister was raped by the military in the street before being killed!' (Interview: 2022MRM3)

Although it was difficult to find any respondents who claimed to be rape victims, I met young girls and women who were victims of groping during body searches. For example, one of the respondents told me,

> A *Tamasud* [a military base/police check post] was set up next to our house. When I took classes, I saw many girls being molested while passing in front of this base. Girls could not walk in the streets. The military always made sure what was inside their clothes, what was not there. Rohingya women had to take off their clothes to show them [the military]! … it was a very horrible thing for us! It is very shameful for us to fix and wear clothes in front of men. When a girl used to go to the market in front of this base, it happened that the military would touch different parts of our body in the name of a clothes or body search. Many others and I have been such victims. It's better to die than have this shame (*beizzot*). (Interview: 2022MRF4)

Buddhists claim that Muslims are waging a 'reproductive jihad'. Citing an academic, Beech (2019, para 47) noted, 'There is this idea of a hyper-fertile Muslim man with his many wives', populating the whole country and eventually taking over the power of the country. Therefore, the ultra-nationalist Buddhist monks have popularised the idea that Rohingya are a dangerously fertile species and will breed many children, thus increasing the Muslim population in the country. This will ultimately threaten Buddhism in Myanmar. As I observed in the Rohingya refugee camps in Bangladesh, the Rohingya family size is larger than the average Bengali family (four/five members in one household). Many families I interviewed consisted of more than eight members. However, during my interviews with Rohingya in the camps, they told me that it was difficult to have more children and multiple wives, as these were strictly controlled by the military; for example, the military even counted how many offspring a goat or cow had. As one of the respondents explained,

> Every year, the military made a list of every family, and according to that, they came to check again later. If a cow gave birth, we had to inform them; we had to get permission and pay money. They always checked us according to the list to see how many members there are in the family. They used to keep a list of the assets and property in our family, so we did not have the right to increase or decrease anything against their will. They controlled everything. (Interview: 2022MRF10)

During their time in Myanmar, reproduction and motherhood was controlled and dependent upon the will of the military authorities who govern the lives of the Rohingya. As one of my respondents explained it,

> From time to time, the military would visit our village, issuing warnings to women not to bear more than two boys. Should a woman exceed this limit, the military would go as far as threatening to harm or kill the additional boys. Furthermore, they advised women against being too intimate [having intercourse] with their husbands, asserting that men should focus solely on working hard to earn a living—nothing beyond that. (Interview: 2022MRM1)

Therefore, Myanmar's gendered social structure constructs men as strong and the protectors of women's livelihood while women's main job is reproduction and easily regulated subject and their bodies can be violated.

Nevertheless, Ma Ba Tha managed to successfully propagate idea that the 'Buddhist women were held up as the symbols of the nation who were in danger of rape by Muslim men' (Beech, 2019, para 47). In fact, Myanmar's armed forces have used rape as a weapon of war in their battles against various ethnic insurgencies. The United Nations has blamed the Myanmar military for 'sexual atrocities reportedly committed in cold blood out of a lethal hatred for the Rohingya' (Beech, 2019, para 48) . Ma Ba Tha monks have rejected such findings and have continued their hate-mongering, even though the group was technically outlawed in 2017. All the interviews I conducted with the Rohingya refugees claimed that rape and physical torture were common weapons of atrocity against them. This stands in contradiction to sentiments like that of the Ma Ba Tha monk, U Rarza, who claimed, 'I don't think anyone would rape Bengali [Rohingya] women because they are ugly and disgusting' (Beech, 2019, para 49) However, in every war and forced displacement, sexual violence has played an integral part, serving as a source of vulnerability to women and men. Numerous studies have demonstrated the detrimental impact of sexual violence on individuals who have experienced it, encompassing adverse effects on their physical and mental well-being, social connections, and economic circumstances (Skjelsbæk, 2001; Freedman, 2016; Féron, 2017; Mack & Na'puti, 2019; Phillimore et al., 2022). Recently, research on sexual violence against men in war and forced displacement has also gained prominence. Some recent research shows that, in selected conflict-affected territories of the eastern Democratic Republic of Congo, approximately 23.6 percent of surveyed men experienced sexual violence; in Liberia, it increased to one-third (32.6 percent) of surveyed men. Sexual violence was also prevalent during the war in the former Yugoslavia (Alexandre et al., 2022). Although sexual violence has predominantly been committed against Rohingya women, it has not been limited to women and girls only; some Burmese, and the military in particular, have also committed sexual violence against men and boys (Women's Refugee Commission, 2018).

Sexual Violence Against Rohingya Men and Boys

Although the focus on sexual violence in conflict and war has been predominantly female-oriented, men and boys have also been victims of such atrocities. During my interviews with male respondents, I found it difficult to get respondents to engage in discussions of sexual violence against men. Some of them felt ashamed of talking about sexual violence against men while they easily talked about rape against Rohingya women. This is, as I argue, connected with the representation of men as powerful, as saviours of female chastity. This is also connected with the social stigma that possibly undermines the image of a man as a protector in the community. However, one of my respondents, who knows at least two men who were sexually assaulted by the military, told me,

> One day, some men were called off to clean the military barracks near our village. After cleaning, the military ordered two young men to stay in the barracks. Accordingly, they had to stay there. In addition, there they became the victims of forced anal sex. They did not tell anyone. As I was very close to them, they just told me. (Interview: 2018MRM7)

During my interviews, many of my respondents agreed that they knew about instances of rape against women where the military tied up their fathers or husbands and then raped the women in front of them. This forced witnessing of performative rape is a devastating form of sexual violence. One of the respondents claimed that witnessing it was worse than being raped. However, during my fieldwork, it was difficult to find any males willing to admit to being sexual victims. Other researchers have pointed out the same issue, claiming that there is a very limited presence of narratives directly articulated by male survivors of sexual violence themselves. Therefore, 'male survivors of sexual violence are pushed away in the limbo of the post-conflict era, as obscene and embarrassing byproducts of war that do not qualify for entering the realm of the political and politicized' (Féron, 2017, p. 63).

In the context of sexual violence against Rohingya males, the Women's Refugee Commission titled their report, '"It's Happening to Our Men as Well": Sexual Violence Against Men and Boys', quoting one of their respondents as saying, 'the same thing that is happening to our women, it's happening to our men as well. It is too shameful to talk about' (Women's Refugee Commission, 2018, p. 10). Sexual violence committed against Rohingya men and boys has included 'forced witnessing of sexual violence against women and girls, genital violence—specifically mutilation, burning, castration, and penis amputation—and anal rape' (Women's Refugee Commission, 2018, p. 9). According to the Women's Refugee Commission (2018), of the total 185 refugee men surveyed in 2017, 10.1 percent reported experiencing rape; 20 percent reported other types of sexual violence, humiliation and sexual abuse; and 8 percent reported witnessing physical or sexual violence.

Why Sexual Violence?

I asked my interviewees why the military committed rape and other forms of sexual violence against them. One of my respondents told me, 'The military sexually assaulted and raped our boys and girls so that we could not even protest against them due to the taboos attached to sexual violence. Therefore, sexual atrocity was an easy tool for the military to force us to leave the country' (Interview: 2022MRM3). Thus, forced witnessing of performative rape by the military and Burmese civilians served as an ethnic cleansing mechanism by inflicting 'terror, humiliation, and anguish on both the female victims and the male observers, and to damage familial bonds, destroy the social fabric, and subjugate communities as whole' (Women's Refugee Commission, 2018, p. 29). However, in recent research, Alam and Wood (2022, p. 1) explored whether sexual violence against the Rohingya was a 'policy (ordered or authorized by commanders) or a practice (driven from below and tolerated by commanders)'. They argued,

[A]t least some elements of the repertoire of sexual violence against the Rohingya were authorized as policy: (1) the regime's long-standing ideological exclusion of the Rohingya from citizenship and its record of demographic engineering to limit their reproduction, (2) the military's policy of ethnic cleansing and commanders' effective control of forces, (3) evidence that the military engages in a distinct pattern of violence against the Rohingya (compared to that against other ethnic minorities, including within northern Rakhine State), particularly the destruction of reproductive capacity and public and performative rape during massacres and forced displacement, and (4) the record of long-standing impunity for and ongoing tolerance of [conflict-related sexual violence]. (Alam & Wood, 2022, p. 15–6)

In a report, Sultana (2018, p. 43) claimed that the Myanmar military raped and committed sexual violence against the Rohingya, where 'army commanders systematically planned and used rape as a weapon against the Rohingya population'.

Gendered Mobility, Discrimination, and Justice

When Rohingya Muslim women were living in Rakhine State, they had limited mobility. They needed permission from the authorities (i.e., local chairpersons) to go to neighbouring areas or townships. They also had almost no access to education and health facilities. Some of the men I interviewed told me they (Rohingya men and women) were able to complete a primary education but were not allowed to go to any higher level than this. However, I found that some Rohingya men had completed higher secondary education, and a few even went to a university in Myanmar.

This form of structural violence against Rohingya women happens on a continuum. Even in the refugee camps, their gender identity restricts their mobility, although they enjoy more freedom in the camps than in Myanmar. This restricted mobility inside the camps grew out of the feeling of insecurity. The refugee women's vulnerability has been revealed when they tried to practice their traditional cultural and Islamic religious practices, such as maintaining '*forda*' (seclusion). They do not want to meet with the males who are not relatives, but maintaining seclusion in the camps is difficult. The women also lack sufficient clothing to maintain '*forda*'. All the women I met/saw in the camps wore a burqa[3] (a form of veil worn by women in many Muslim societies). However, one of my respondents told me she has to borrow a burqa from her neighbour when she needs to go to collect food aid. I observed that whenever I asked why they have so many children, one of them said, 'If Allah wants, what we can do? As Allah gave us the children, He will feed them' (Interview: 2022MRF7). Many of them do not know about contraception and depend on their husband for reproductive choices. Several studies have examined the issue of contraception and birth control among the Rohingya refugees living in the camps in Bangladesh (Islam et al., 2021a, 2021b; Khan et al., 2021; Islam & Habib, 2024). Of note, Islam and Habib (2024, p. 2) found that

> contraceptive use among Rohingya refugees was constrained by various socio-cultural and religious beliefs. The desire for a larger number of children to ensure the continuity of the lineage and to be able to contribute to the growth of the Islamic population serves as a major barrier. Lack of decision making power regarding reproductive life not only stops participation but also makes women vulnerable to IPV [intimate partner violence] and marriage dissolution within the camps. Moreover, the fear of side effects, such as a particular method would cause infertility, discourages women from using contraception. Many of these fears stem from myths, misconceptions, and mistrust in the existing medical system.

During my camp visits, I observed several children playing with condoms as a toy, indicating an inappropriate use of contraception by the refugees.

Women who become victims of gender-based violence inside the camps do not receive formal justice, as the Rohingya lack formal refugee status in Bangladesh. They rely on the *Majhi* and Rohingya community elders, as well as some refugee-led organisations (RLOs), for dispute resolution, mostly on a small scale. Rohingya women said that the injustice was worse in Rakhine State as they have never received any justice for what the Magh did to them, be it sexual violence or other types of violence. The state of Myanmar extends justice only to citizens. As the Rohingya are not considered citizens, they are denied such services. The military (Tatmadaw)—the largest perpetrator of sexual violence—is exempt from the justice system. For example, Office of the United Nations High Commissioner for Human Rights (2019, p. 53) explains,

> In Myanmar, there are limited accountability mechanisms in place for addressing sexual and gender-based violations. There is legislative impunity for sexual assault and other violations perpetrated by the Tatmadaw: soldiers are protected under article 381 of the Constitution, which suspends the right to justice in times of emergency. The Ministry of Defence is not subject to civilian control, meaning that the military operates with very little civilian oversight or accountability. Survivors of sexual and gender-based violence have no recourse to justice.

Intermarriage, Women, and the Monks

Ultranationalist leaders and followers of Ma Ba Tha have claimed that Muslim men are forcibly marrying Buddhist women, which will result in the decline of the Buddhist population, ultimately threatening Buddhist nationhood. All of my Rohingya interviewees denied the accusation that Rohingya men have been forcibly marrying and forcibly converting any Buddhist women to Islam. Some of them knew of Rohingya boys who married Buddhist girls, but they were not forced. When I asked about forced marriage, my respondents told me, 'No, no, no ..., it is not happening that Rohingyas are forcibly marrying a Buddhist girl. However, there are many cases where they are marrying willingly, meaning two people are marrying by consent. However, there are also examples of Magh forcibly marrying Muslim girls' (Interview: 2022MRM1). Another respondent told me that intermarriage is not easy:

> When two people become friends or fall in love with each other, then if both of them want to get married, then there are some cases of marriage between Rohingya boys and Buddhist girls. However, it is not easy. Because it is not legal in Myanmar, if you want to do this kind of marriage in Myanmar, you must go to jail, and the Myanmar government never allows it. Even if you want to have such a marriage there, no permission is given whether a Rohingya boy or a Buddhist girl desired so. (Interview: 2022MRM3)

When asked how intermarriage is still occurring, he replied,

> In that case, it can be seen that in some cases, the boy might be fleeing to Bangladesh with the girl, or else he would go to the hilly area and live in such a way that no one knows them or shows suspicion about them or can inform about them. (Interview: 2022MRM3)

Thus, it can be said that intermarriage, though not forceful, is occurring among Rohingya men and Buddhist women. This has had implications for marriage regulation acts by the state of Myanmar. Ultranationalist Buddhists, and especially Ma Ba Tha—which considered intermarriage a threat to Buddhism, were important actors in the passing of restrictive laws. 'The Buddhist Women's Special Marriage Law', part of a package of four so-called Race and Religion Protection Laws, was passed by the Myanmar parliament in 2015. This new law made it hard for Buddhist women to marry outside their religion (Beech, 2019). Moreover, 'all four bills raise serious human rights concerns. The Population Control Law … empowers authorities to limit the number of children members of any designated group can have, opening the possibility of discriminatory actions against religious or ethnic minorities' (Human Rights Watch, 2015, para 10). As part of Ma Ba Tha's move against intermarriage, it collected 2.5 million signatures in favour of its march against interreligious marriage (Walton & Hayward, 2014). Consequently, Ma Ba Tha proposed a draft marriage bill to the government in 2013 and the government released a slightly modified version of the bill in late 2014 (Human Rights Watch, 2015). Because many Buddhist women also supported these ultranationalist laws, it is important to know why.

Buddhist Women in the Ultranationalist Movement

As some authors argued, ultranationalist movements such as Ma Ba Tha have popularity not only among educated Buddhists but also at the grassroots level. When a vacuum was created by the end of military rule in Myanmar, organisations such as Ma Ba Tha came forward to fill it, as no others were able to do. Ma Ba Tha gained popularity among the grassroots Buddhists due to its activities for the 'promotion and protection of Buddhism' (International Crisis Group, 2017, p. 20). Some of the activities include promoting shared Buddhist cultural values, providing a social safety net (taking care of the poor, sick and elderly; providing food and health care; etc.), disaster relief, education for underprivileged and rural youth through their Dhamma School, dispute resolution, 'women's rights', and legal aid. These activities are similar to those of many other faith-based (or militant) organisations (Salehin, 2016). Although they see the protection of women as a religious duty, Ma Ba Tha has been criticised for their activities against Muslims and women from other religious backgrounds. As mentioned earlier, Ma Ba Tha's role in enacting the Marriage Regulation Act curtailed the rights of women from other religions. However, Ma Ba Tha has numerous supporters amongst Buddhist women and, as one estimate shows, anywhere between 20,000 to 80,000 women in Yangon have become members and the central Mandalay area has approximately 3000 female members. The number of informal followers and participants is likely much higher (Marler & Aguilar, 2018).

The puzzling question is: why do Buddhist women support this patriarchal, violent, and ultranationalist group? One way to address this issue is to focus on the social structure and the status of women in Myanmar. A famous Buddhist feminist nun argues that 'Burma has a male-dominated, patriarchal society, which means religious life is also dominated by men. The patriarchy is deep-rooted here' (Rigby, 2017, para 2). In such a patriarchal context, where women are often marginalised, Ma Ba Tha provides 'opportunities' that women do not always find elsewhere. Those who join Ma Ba Tha contribute to a variety of roles in the organisation, including managing administration (e.g., managing donations, communications, or keeping historical records), teaching in Dhamma School (including Sunday school), and other community outreach programmes (Marler & Aguilar, 2018). This gives many women an opportunity to enhance their agency in the public sphere. It is not only the underprivileged and rural women who have become members of the organisation but also nuns, female religious scholars, lawyers, educators, medical professionals, and other tertiary-level students. Based on interviews with female members, the International Crisis Group (ICG) suggested that the rise of feminism in Myanmar is a reason for joining Ma Ba Tha. As mentioned earlier, Ma Ba Tha claims to protect women as part of its religious duty (International Crisis Group, 2017) and 'the support of female nationalists stems primarily from a commitment to outlaw polygamy and strongly felt concerns over forced conversion, which they see as the likely (if not inevitable) byproduct of Muslim-Buddhist marriages' (International Crisis Group, 2017, p. 13). It is, therefore, clear that Ma Ba Tha's mass mobilisation to pass a set of rules concerning marriage and the protection of religion serves to 'empower' and 'protect' Buddhist women while dehumanising Rohingya Muslim women.

OTHER FORMS OF VIOLENCE

Alongside physical violence and the burning down the Rohingya property, the military has also committed religious violence. One of the respondents (Interview: 2022MRM3) said:

> They [Magh] do not allow us to go to the Mosque, *waaj* [Islamic preaching]; they don't allow us to pray. If we do want to perform these, Magh starts violence against us. They don't even allow us to offer Eid prayer and funeral prayer. ... when they come into our house, if they don't find any male member of the family, they torture the women and particularly the young women. They physically torture them and rape them. When they leave our house, they also take our cattle with them.

All of my respondents claimed that the military could take any Rohingya person from their home and could do anything with/to them, including forced labour, physical and mental torture, and rape. One of my respondents told me,

> When we were in Rakhine State, boys were tortured and girls were tortured. Boys were taken to various military stations or police stations to work. One hundred people were taken every day from our village to the police barracks. They were forced to clean their gardens, cut grass, and water gardens. We used to be treated like slaves. If anyone did not want to go, they were beaten, and sometimes the military would come and take whoever they found on the way to cut grass for their pet cows and goats. They did not care whether the Rohingya person they were taking was educated, uneducated, or qualified to do these things. Moreover, sometimes the military would get drunk, beat up the person on the way, then enter the neighbourhood and take away the beautiful girls from their homes, keeping them for two to three days. Even if anyone won't listen to them, these people have been tortured and killed. (Interview: 2022MRM1)

CONCLUSION

It is now well documented that Myanmar has committed various atrocities against the Rohingya minority, including murder and sexual violence. In everyday life, the Rohingya have been systematically discriminated against, with women being treated the worst. Rohingya women have faced a double burden in Myanmar: physical violence, mental torture, and other forms of oppression by the military, monks, and ordinary Maghs, on the one hand, and the patriarchal Rohingya social structure, on the other. Therefore, structural violence in the forms of discrimination (e.g., in education) and pervasive poverty have affected women, men, and children in different ways. A gendered 'threat' narrative has been systematically disseminated among the ordinary populace in Rakhine State and Myanmar through diverse social media, including Facebook, and tangible media, such as newspapers, CDs, and DVDs. These narratives have been constructed and perpetuated by various actors, prominently including Buddhist monks. They delineate female Rohingyas as dangerously reproductive entities who pose a demographic threat to Buddhism through the potential proliferation of the Muslim population. Therefore, Rohingya motherhood, reproduction, and sexuality were threatened and controlled by the military. Conversely, the image of Rohingya men has been constructed as a 'threat' to nationalism, identity, and religion (through forced marriage and conversion of Buddhist women). These factors have led to the justification of different forms of violence against the Rohingya, including sexual violence. Targeted efforts aimed specifically at undermining Rohingya girls and women's reproductive capacities, as well as instances of the public and performative raping of Rohingya women, attest to an enduring culture of abuse and impunity perpetuated by the Myanmar military. Sexual violence, wielded as a weapon, serves the strategic purpose of disrupting the essential facets of Rohingya femininity, motherhood, and reproductive capabilities. It precipitates trauma and stigma within the community, thereby eroding its societal fabric. Consequently, the Rohingya have been forced into displacement, seeking refuge in camps within Bangladesh where they continue to be victims of different forms of direct, structural, cultural, and symbolic violence. The ensuing chapter undertakes an exploration of the gendered vulnerabilities intrinsic to the context of the Cox's Bazar refugee camps in Bangladesh.

NOTES

1. See for detail, https://democracy-reporting.org/buddhist-nationalists-used-facebook-to-fuel-hate-speech-in-myanmar/
2. In 2013, the US *Time* magazine featured Ashin Wirathu on their front cover, displaying a photograph of him and captioning it with the title 'The face of Buddhist terror', and calling him 'Buddhist Bin Laden'. See the *Time* magazine vol. 182, no.1 that made a front-cover page entitled 'The Face of Buddhist Terror', July 1, 2013.
3. There are some misconceptions regarding the use of the burqa as an Islamic tradition among scholars in Islam. Quranic verses talk about modesty and covering the body parts. For example, in Al-Qur'an, surah An-Nur, verse 31 clearly states, 'And tell the believing women to subdue their eyes, and maintain their chastity. They shall not reveal any parts of their bodies, except that which is apparent. They shall cover their chests with their "khimar". The use of the burqa is rather socially constructed. It is a choice, a style by Muslims in some countries. "Islam is not concerned with the style as long as it fulfills the basic requirement of niqab"', Chowdhury, N., Bakar, H. and Elmetwally, A. (2017). 'Misconception of Islamic Apparel, Niqab: A Phenomenological Approach.' *Malaysian Journal of Communication* 33(4): 204–217.

REFERENCES

Alam, M., & Wood, E. J. (2022). Ideology and the Implicit Authorization of Violence as Policy: The Myanmar Military's Conflict-Related Sexual Violence against the Rohingya. *Journal of global security studies, 7*(2).

Alexandre, A. B., Rutega, B., Byamungu, P. A., Notia, C. A., & Alldén, S. (2022). A Man Never Cries: Barriers to Holistic Care for Male Survivors of Sexual Violence in Eastern DRC. *Medicine, Conflict and Survival, 38*(2), 116–139.

BBC. (2018). *The Country Where Facebook Posts Whipped Up Hate.* BBC. https://www.bbc.com/news/blogs-trending-45449938, accessed on January 9, 2020.

Beech, H. (2019). Buddhists Go to Battle: When Nationalism Overrides Pacifism. *The New York Times.*

Bookbinder, A. (2013). 969: The Strange Numerological Basis for Burma's Religious Violence. *The Atlantic.* https://www.theatlantic.com/international/archive/2013/04/969-the-strange-numerological-basis-for-burmas-religious-violence/274816/, accessed on 28 March 2020.

Bowser, M. J. (2021). Buddhism Has Been Insulted. Take Immediate Steps: Burmese Fascism and the Origins of Burmese Islamophobia, 1936–38. *Modern Asian Stud, 55*(4), 1112–1150.

Chowdhury, N. A., Bakar, H. S. A., & Elmetwally, A. A. (2017). Misconception of Islamic Apparel, Niqab: A Phenomenological Approach. *Malaysian Journal of Communication, 33*(4), 204–217.

Croft, S. (2012). *Securitizing Islam: Identity and the Search for Security.* Cambridge University Press.

Das, V. (2008). Violence, Gender, and Subjectivity. *Annual Review of Anthropology, 37*(1), 283–299.

Egreteau, R. (2011). Burmese Indians in Contemporary Burma: Heritage, Influence, and Perceptions Since 1988. *Asian Ethnicity, 12*(1), 33–54.

Féron, É. (2017). Wartime Sexual Violence Against Men Why So Oblivious? *European Review of International Studies, 4*(1), 60–74.

Fink, C. (2018). Dangerous Speech, Anti-Muslim Violence, and Facebook in Myanmar. *Journal of International Affairs, 71*(1.5), 43–52.

Freedman, J. (2016). Sexual and Gender-Based Violence Against Refugee Women: A Hidden Aspect of the Refugee "Crisis". *Reproductive Health Matters, 24*(47), 18–26.

Fuller, T. (2013). Extremism Rises Among Myanmar Buddhists. *The New York Times.* https://www.nytimes.com/2013/06/21/world/asia/extremism-rises-among-myanmar-buddhists-wary-of-muslim-minority.html, accessed on April 6, 2018.

Gallimore, R. B. (2008). Militarism, Ethnicity, and Sexual Violence in the Rwandan Genocide. *Feminist Africa, 10,* 9–30.

Head, J. (2017, September 11). Rohingya Crisis: Seeing Through the Official Story in Myanmar. *BBC.*

Human Rights Watch (2015). *Burma: Reject Discriminatory Marriage Bill*. Human Rights Watch. https://www.hrw.org/news/2015/07/09/burma-reject-discriminatory-marriage-bill, accessed on May 7, 2019.

Ibrahimi, N. (2022). Rumor and Collective Action Frames: An Assessment of How Competing Conceptions of Gender, Culture, and Rule of Law Shaped Responses to Rumor and Violence in Afghanistan. *Studies in conflict and terrorism, 45*(1), 20–42.

International Crisis Group. (2017). *Buddhism and State Power in Myanmar. Asia Report No.290*.

Islam, M., & Habib, S. E. (2024). "I Don't Want My Marriage to End": A Qualitative Investigation of the Sociocultural Factors Influencing Contraceptive Use Among Married Rohingya Women Residing in Refugee Camps in Bangladesh. *Reproductive Health, 21*(1), 32.

Islam, M. M., Hossain, M. A., & Yunus, M. Y. (2021a). Why Is the Use of Contraception So Low Among the Rohingya Displaced Population in Bangladesh? *The Lancet Regional Health–Western Pacific, 13*.

Islam, M. M., Khan, M. N., & Rahman, M. M. (2021b). Factors Affecting Child Marriage and Contraceptive Use Among Rohingya Girls in Refugee Camps. *The Lancet Regional Health–Western Pacific, 12*.

Johnson, M. S. (1998). *Gender & History, 10*(2): 252–277.

Khan, M. N., Islam, M. M., Rahman, M. M., & Rahman, M. M. (2021). Access to Female Contraceptives by Rohingya Refugees, Bangladesh. *Bulletin of the World Health Organization, 99*(3), 201.

Mack, A. N., & Na'puti, T. R. (2019). "Our Bodies Are Not Terra Nullius": Building a Decolonial Feminist Resistance to Gendered Violence. *Women's Studies in Communication, 42*(3), 347–370.

Marler, I., & Aguilar, M. (2018). *What's Attracting Women to Myanmar's Buddhist Nationalist Movement?* OpenDemocracy. https://www.opendemocracy.net/en/5050/women-myanmar-buddhist-nationalist-movement/, accessed on May 6, 2020.

McCarthy, G., & Menager, J. (2017). Gendered Rumours and the Muslim Scapegoat in Myanmar's Transition. *Journal of Contemporary Asia, 47*(3), 396–412.

Meta. (2018). *Removing Myanmar Military Officials From Facebook*. https://about.fb.com/news/2018/08/removing-myanmar-officials/, accessed on March 23, 2019.

Office of the United Nations High Commissioner for Human Rights. (2019, September 9–27). *Sexual and Gender-Based Violence in Myanmar and the Gendered Impact of Its Ethnic Conflicts, Office of the United Nations High Commissioner for Human Rights*. Human Rights Council Forty second session. Agenda item4.

Okech, A. (2021). Gender and State-Building Conversations: The Discursive Production of Gender Identity in Kenya and Rwanda. *Conflict, Security & Development*, 21(4), 501–515.

Phillimore, J., Pertek, S., Akyuz, S., Darkal, H., Hourani, J., McKnight, P., Ozcurumez, S., & Taal, S. (2022). "We Are Forgotten": Forced Migration, Sexual and Gender-Based Violence, and Coronavirus Disease-2019. *Violence Against Women*, 28(9), 2204–2230.

Rigby, J. (2017). Meet Burma's Feminist Buddhist Nun. *Tricycle: The Buddhist Review*. https://tricycle.org/trikedaily/meet-burmas-feminist-nun/, accessed on April 24, 2020.

Salehin, M. M. (2016). *Islamic NGOs in Bangladesh: Development, Piety and Neoliberal Governmentality*. Routledge.

SBS. (2013). *Matra of Rage*. on SBS. https://www.sbs.com.au/news/dateline/tvepisode/mantra-of-rage, accessed on April 21, 2018.

Skjelsbæk, I. (2001). Sexual Violence and War: Mapping Out a Complex Relationship. *European Journal of International Relations*, 7(2), 211–237.

Sultana, R. (2018). *Rape by Command Sexual Violence as a Weapon Against the Rohingya*. Chittagong.

Walton, M. J., & Hayward, S. (2014). *Contesting Buddhist Narratives: Democratization, Nationalism, and Communal Violence in Myanmar Policy Studies (Southeast Asia)* (p. 71). Honolulu, East–West Center.

Women's Refugee Commission. (2018). *"It's Happening to Our Men as Well": Sexual Violence Against Rohingya Men and Boys*. Women's Refugee Commission. https://www.womensrefugeecommission.org/research-resources/its-happening-to-our-men-as-well/, accessed on November 7, 2021.

Open Access This chapter is licensed under the terms of the Creative Commons Attribution 4.0 International License (http://creativecommons.org/licenses/by/4.0/), which permits use, sharing, adaptation, distribution and reproduction in any medium or format, as long as you give appropriate credit to the original author(s) and the source, provide a link to the Creative Commons license and indicate if changes were made.

The images or other third party material in this chapter are included in the chapter's Creative Commons license, unless indicated otherwise in a credit line to the material. If material is not included in the chapter's Creative Commons license and your intended use is not permitted by statutory regulation or exceeds the permitted use, you will need to obtain permission directly from the copyright holder.

CHAPTER 5

Gendered Vulnerabilities and Violence in Rohingya Refugee Camps in Bangladesh

Abstract This chapter discusses the various vulnerabilities and violence that refugees experience in the refugee camps in Bangladesh. It argues that Rohingya women continue to bear the scars of violence experienced in Myanmar, exacerbated by the patriarchal and traditional structure of the Rohingya community, resulting in shame, psychological stress, and domestic violence inside the camps. Some victims of domestic violence and husbands' multiple marriages perceive these practices as justified and part of their daily lives, representing symbolic violence. This chapter illustrates how child marriage for girls is used as a negative coping mechanism, while multiple marriages committed by men are viewed as a form of 'business'. It also argues that access to justice and everyday safety and well-being are gendered. Furthermore, a gendered form of othering is evident, where Rohingya men are constructed as the 'monstrous other', while women are portrayed as victims and vulnerable.

Keywords Violence • Child marriage • Multiple marriage • Negative coping • Justice • Security • Othering • Refugee camps

Introduction

Whereas the Rohingya faced fierce violence in Myanmar, they continue to face multidimensional vulnerabilities in the Rohingya refugee camps in Cox's Bazar in Bangladesh. Five years after their forced displacement, they

© The Author(s) 2024
M. M. Salehin, *Gendered Vulnerabilities and Violence in Forced Migration*, https://doi.org/10.1007/978-3-031-62435-3_5

69

still bear mental trauma, the physical scars of violence, shame, stigma, and fear related to sexual violence. The precarious conditions in the camps are forcing this traumatised population to live a 'bare life' (Agamben, 1998). In the camps, men tend to be overall less vulnerable while women and children tend to be more vulnerable. One of my respondents made this sentiment clear when she said, 'Being female is fearful ... it is dangerous to be a woman' (Interview: 2022MRF4). The dimensions of such vulnerabilities are multifaceted and dependent on intersectional identities, i.e., gender, age, power, education, access to resources (human and financial), and community structure. This chapter discusses such vulnerabilities, as well as the different forms of structural, cultural, and symbolic violence in the refugee camps, and the complexities intertwined in intersectional gender identity.

FROM SHAMING AND IGNORANCE TO DOMESTIC VIOLENCE

The patriarchal and traditional structure of the Rohingya community, which is also prevalent in the camps in Bangladesh, has led to shame, stigma, and different types of gender-based violence (GBV) against Rohingya women in the camps. Some of my respondents who worked as health workers in the camps told me their experiences dealing with abortions they had performed for the women and girls who became pregnant, due to rape mainly, by the Myanmar military while they were in Rakhine State. One of the respondents explained:

> I work for MSF's gender-based violence project where I have performed abortions on approximately 122 such pregnant women. Most of them were unmarried and very good looking. What would they teach the child they would give birth to, and what would be the paternity of the child if an unmarried girl had a child without paternity? Then, there would be no chance for them to get married later. Tell me, don't they have a life too? (Interview: 2022MRF4)

However, it was not easy to perform the abortion. My respondent told me,

> These girls were raped and consequently became pregnant. Now, if they give birth to the baby, then will any man in the world ever marry them? Of course not! Most of the girls were one month, two months, or three months

pregnant. We have built a very good relationship with those girls, saying different things like abortion cannot be done after three months, you have to bring the baby into the world, you are like my sister and friend, we are doing everything because we thought about your well-being. They trust us, and we did abortions by keeping these very secret. However, some girls became pregnant due to rape and did not tell anyone, even their parents. Even when the parents knew about it, they also denied telling us about the pregnancy. Because they thought that their daughter's future would be ruined, no one would marry their daughter, and people would humiliate them. You know, we must live in this community. (Interview: 2022MRF4)

As their futures were the most important concern for the parents and the girls themselves, I asked my respondents how society treats them now. One of my respondents replied,

We have done it [abortion], so we kept it secret. Secrecy is still prevalent in camps, and it is related to the welfare of victims of sexual violence. We, as volunteers, also feel responsible for keeping it secret. We shouldn't let the news about the victims spread in the community to make her life more vulnerable. (Interview: 2022MRF5)

The same respondents also claimed that women and men in the camps tend to hide other forms of violence committed, particularly by men against women. I asked her why they hide it. She replied, 'it is because women often are not allowed by their male members to report it to the *Majhi*, or CiC [Camp-in-Charge]. I think this is related to our cultural norms regarding women's behaviour in public, as well as the dependency of women on the male for everything' (Interview: 2023MRF1). This illustrates how traditional gender norms and social structure exacerbate structural violence among the Rohingya (Galtung, 1996).

Previous research and news reports have discussed the prevalence of different kinds of GBV in the Rohingya refugee camps, including physical torture. One study claimed that the main perpetrator of violence against women is intimate partners; for example, approximately 81 percent of violence against women was committed by their intimate partners (International Rescue Committee, 2020). Although it was difficult to know the extent of such domestic violence in the camps, one of my respondents, who works in an NGO as a social worker and deals with domestic violence, told me, 'I have 20–25 such cases of domestic violence in my hands. Some days ago, one husband punched on his wife's face and broke his wife's tooth ... It is not very uncommon in other households in the camps'. Other types of violence against women in the camps, as my respondents told me, include denial and deprived access to resources and services (e.g., control of food and other aid, controlling movement). Another aspect of domestic violence is psychological harm and abuse (e.g., insults, humiliation, and threats). There is also evidence of sexual violence by intimate partners in the form of forced intercourse among married Rohingya women.

I asked my respondents why a male member of the family commits such violence against a female member of the family. The main reasons they offered for domestic violence against females are early marriage, lack of education, the incapacity of women and their families to meet the dowry demands, multiple marriages among the men, and lack of income or jobs for men. Moreover, as the Rohingya social structure is patriarchal and lacks access to resources, there is a high level of inequality between males and females. As is evident from the different stories shared by the respondent, a man in the patriarchal Rohingya society is expected to be the main breadwinner and protect his family from the shock. Being a refugee in the camp who is not entitled to work makes it difficult to sustain a livelihood. Therefore, the man feels powerless and a sense of guilt not being able to feed his family. This stressor also contributes to violence against female member of the family.

One of my respondents did not see it as violence against her; rather, it has been the tradition of the community, and 'the husband has the right to physically torture his wife if she doesn't listen to him' (Interview: 2018MRF6). When asked why she thinks so, she replied, 'My husband provides me with food and clothes and fulfils my basic needs. Therefore, I should be obedient to him and follow whatever he demands. In addition, if I fail to follow him, he can punish me'. This resonates with what Bourdieu (1979) calls 'symbolic violence', in which women do not see or recognise domestic violence as violence in any form. However, this attitude was not prevalent among the women I interviewed, as many of my female respondents were on the way to being empowered. Here, I refer to those refugee women who obtained some education in Myanmar and now work as paid volunteers in different organisations, and who are increasingly becoming aware of gender discrimination and the ways to achieve gender equity.

It became obvious from the respondents that domestic violence against women is widespread in the camps. Alongside domestic violence, different forms of structural violence—for example, child marriage and multiple marriages—have continued in the camps in Bangladesh. The section that follows explains child marriage and multiple marriages in camps.

MULTIPLE MARRIAGES, CHILD MARRIAGES, AND HIGH FERTILITY

From news reports and information provided by the Government of Bangladesh (GoB), there is a prevalence of high birth rates, multiple marriages, and child marriages in the refugee camps. According to GoB, every year, approximately 30,000 children are born in camps.[1] The GoB estimates that, in 2022, 95 children were born every day in the camps in Cox's Bazar. I, too, found a large family size among my respondents and asked them why there was such a high population growth rate in the camps. One common answer was that children are Allah's will. Recently, the Bangladeshi Home Minister commented that Rohingyas have more children to obtain more food aid since the headcount, not one's age, is considered in the allocation of food aid for refugees (Radio Free Asia, 2022). However, subjective notions about religion or the desire for more food cannot explain the population growth in the camps. Rather, several interlinked structural factors are responsible for this rapid growth. For example, all of my respondents agreed that it was not easy to have or give birth to more children in Rakhine State, as the military and the local administration have enormous control over births, not only with children but also with livestock.

Fewer reproductive restrictions in the camps is one factor. One of my respondents told me, 'Coming to Bangladesh gave us a lot of freedom and Bangladesh has done a lot of good things for us. There is no control from the government on the birth of children. Therefore, many of our Rohingya people are giving birth to more children than ever before' (Interview: 2022MRF4). Other factors contributing to the increased birth rate in the camps include multiple marriages, child marriage, and the lack of women's agency. One of my respondents explained how the lack of women's agency contributes to a high birth rate. She told me, 'I have no control over giving birth. We haven't been taking any birth control measures. Even when I was introduced to birth control measures by one NGO here in the camp, my husband insisted not to use them'. Then, I asked why not, and she replied, 'I can't tell you the reason...I feel ashamed' (Interview: 2018MRF3). Taboos, lack of education, and social stigma related to birth control collectively influence or shape people's perceptions about birth control among the Rohingya, particularly among women. This is connected with the control of women's sexual and reproductive choices by men and regulating the use of women's bodies by men which serves as a pivotal and defining aspect of patriarchy (Whisnant, 2021).

In addition to fewer reproductive restrictions and the lack of women's agency, child marriages and multiple marriages are contributing factors. In the camps, there are many incidences of multiple marriages. One of my respondents told me how men justify their multiple marriages: 'Many of our Rohingya people think that our Prophet Mohammad (SWA), married twelve times, so why cannot we get married multiple times, many people think that should one of their wives become sick, they will need to marry another to serve them' (Interview: 2022MRF8). This can be considered a type of cultural violence because, in this instance, men use religion to justify their multiple marriages (*beshi-biya*).[2] Although Rohingya women generally have a negative view of multiple marriages, some women misrecognise it as a form of violence (symbolic violence) (Bourdieu & Wacquant, 2004) and try to justify it with necessity (*zorurot óiye*). For example, when asked if she knows anyone who has multiple marriages, one respondent replied with a big laugh, 'I have it in my house. My father married twice'. She then added that 'it was for a valid reason. My mother went to jail, and there was no one to take care of and cook for us... Now my two mothers happily live under the same roof. No fighting between them. We are eight siblings from my mother's side and two from my stepmother's side' (Interview: 2022MRF2). Moreover, the misrecognition of violence by Rohingya women may also be connected to class position, education, and access to resources.

Respondents also noted that it was not easy to attain multiple wives and more kids while in Rakhine State. One of them told me,

> We had to take a *Zati* photo (a photo of all the family members together). In Myanmar, we could not get married multiple times.[3] We could not get married before turning 18 years old. If someone wanted to get married, they had to go to the military camp to get married. We were forced to get married in a way that we had to confirm in the marriage contract (*Nikah*) that we would not seek multiple marriages. They made sure that I was above 18 years old, and they forced us to pay the groom a very high bride money so that the groom could not divorce and get married again. (Interview: 2022MRF5)

This is a control mechanism to ensure that the Rohingya population would not increase. As discussed in the previous chapter, mainstream Buddhists and the military in Myanmar consider the Rohingya to be 'dangerously reproductive', which in turn would populate the country with Muslims.

One of the respondents gave an interesting insight into multiple marriages. She thinks that 'getting married is a job. As most of the Rohingya young men do not have any job at the camps or are not involved in any productive work, they think what they can do is get married' (Interview: 2022MRM12). Other respondents connected multiple marriages with the financial benefits. One interviewee discussed the dowry (*zotok*) tradition, which is widely practiced in camps, noting, 'it's not only cash payment but also gold (what they have brought, mainly from Rakhine) or any other material goods that can be paid as dowry. Therefore, someone who got married in Camp 1 can go to Camp 20 to get married there to live on the dowry for days' (Interview: 2022MRM9). Another respondent observed that, when a man marries a woman, he becomes the owner of the woman and everything belonging to her. This also affects the number of ration cards they receive and he then has control over these rationed goods. My respondents identified additional factors that are responsible for multiple marriages. One such factor is the lack of livelihood activities for male refugees in the camps. As they are not legally allowed to work, they sit idle. There is also a lack of recreational facilities in the camps, so men spend a lot of time sitting in front of small shops in the camps and gossiping. One respondent considered multiple marriages to be a 'negative coping mechanism' to the vulnerabilities faced by male refugees (Interview: 2023INGOF1). Few of my respondents claimed that by nature men are polygamous and thus 'because of this bad habit wherever he goes and sees a beautiful woman, he gets married with that woman' (Interview: 2022MRF8).

Child marriage violates human rights and it limits or inhibits the growth of girls to their full potential. Nonetheless, all of my respondents, along with several recent studies, have mentioned a high prevalence of child marriage in camps (Melnikas et al., 2020; Oxfam International, 2018; UNFPA, 2020). Data published by the Myanmar Demographic and Health Survey (DHS) for 2015–2016 showed that 16 percent of girls were married before the age of 18 and 1.9 percent were married before the age of 15 nationwide (Myanmar Ministry of Health and Sports and ICF, 2017). Although the prevalence of child marriage was not given for

Rakhine State and specifically for the Rohingya, my interviewees told me about the occurrence of child marriage in their community. It was not easy to conduct child marriages in Rakhine State and, those who did had to bribe the local authority and the military. However, the situation in the camp is different. I asked my respondents why there is a prevalence of child marriage in the camps. One told me that the traditional and religious structure of the Rohingya community that is responsible. She said,

> In our Rohingya community, when a girl becomes big (*Dōr oiye*), we cannot delay marrying our girls, as the boys will start looking at them. Many people say bad things about the girls, and sometimes these might be fake. Our community directly or indirectly pushes us to marry our girls early. (Interview: 2022MRF2)

Then, I asked when a girl is considered 'becoming big' and eligible for marriage. She replied, 'with the start of her first menstruation (*haiz shuru'on*) of a girl, in our community, people start to think about her marriage. However, the eligibility for boys is different, and in most cases, a boy's eligibility for marriage is connected to his ability to earn'.

All the respondents agreed that the lack of education and poverty is responsible for child marriage. However, there are those who object to child marriage among the Rohingya, as one of my respondents told me,

> I am now 19 years old and unmarried. If I were from another family, I was supposed to be married when I turned 12 or 13 years old. However, my mother did not do that as she understood that setting marriage for a very young girls in not healthy and safe. As I got the opportunity to study here and live in the city [Cox's Bazar], it also has an impact on not getting married early. However, most importantly, early marriages vary from family to family and by educational and economic background. (Interview: 2022MRF7)

Other gender-specific aspects of child marriage stream from feelings of insecurity. Insecurity comes in the form of being susceptible to physical or sexual violence by males in camps. When asked what kinds of insecurity women experience, one interviewee replied,

> Child marriage occurs due not only to poverty but also to different kinds of insecurity in the camps. For example, when we pass through a road, even a very adult male teases us. Sometimes some adult males abduct females in the camps. In the camps, it has become so fierce that we had to hide even a very

young girl child. One is abducting another's young girls, disregarding whether she is young or adult age. Therefore, marrying her to others is a way to get rid of such problems. (Interview: 2022MRF8)

Another respondent told me, 'When our girls turn 11 years old, parents start off setting their marriage and within a year they must complete it. It's a relief for the parents'. When asked why this was so, she replied, 'In one family, if there are three/four girls staying idle at home, parents are in constant fear. Fear of many things. Fear of what others will say about their unmarried girls, fear about how to feed all these girls and fear of teasing by a male in the camps. Additionally, a parent can empty the crowded space in their house getting their girls married as early as possible' (Interview: 2023MRF7).

Due to the lack of space in the camps, large numbers of people are stuck living together. It is interesting to know how lack of space has contributed to child marriage as a negative coping mechanism. As another respondent explained,

> In our camp, our houses are tiny. In such a small house, it is impossible to accommodate a large family. For example, in my family, we are seven members, and the house size is 10 yards (appx. 9 sq. meters). Where will my parents sleep, where will my brother sleep and where will his wife sleep? Just imagine the situation when parents, adult girls, and their brothers and in-laws have to sleep in a very small space and under the same roof. In such a 10-yard house, we all are living jam-packed like a sack of potatoes. No privacy, no intimacy, it is just a disaster. It is not a human life, but something else. No space to breathe here! In other camps, there are more specious houses. Therefore, I have seen in my camp, that parents are coping with the scarcity of space by getting rid of their daughters by arranging early marriage for them. (Interview: 2022MRF8)

It is crucial to comprehend the complex dynamics and the interplay between subjective interpretations of religion, notions of piety, and the instrumental use of Islam as a means to justify one's actions. This becomes evident when examining the justifications articulated by the Rohingya community, where the practice of multiple marriages, for instance, is often attributed to the example of the Prophet of Islam and his multiple marriages. However, a discrepancy arises when Rohingya men abandon their sick wives and neglect their children, contradicting the teachings and actions (Sunnah) of the Prophet. In such instances, individuals seek to manipulate the religious beliefs of the ordinary Rohingya, exploiting Islam to provide legitimacy for their actions and to fulfil their personal needs.

With regard to the issue of multiple marriages, there is insufficient governmental and international organisational intervention. According to some respondents, obtaining permission from the Camp-in-Charge (CiC)[4] to marry within the camps takes around a year. As a result, Rohingya men opt to marry with the assistance of camp elders, avoiding the expenses that the bride's parents would otherwise incur during the waiting period for CiC approval. During the marriage process, the groom and his relatives traditionally visit the bride's home until the completion of the marriage ceremony. Thus, if CiC approval is delayed, the bride's parents would need to entertain a larger number of guests during that time. Consequently, parents find it more practical to organise marriage without the CiC's permission.

FROM PERSONAL HYGIENE TO MENTAL TRAUMA

During the interviews, it was evident that refugees suffer from different diseases and mental trauma. All the respondents, regardless of their gender identity, told me they are still bearing mental trauma from their forced relocation and current precarious living situation. For example, one respondent said,

> The girls who are inside the house suffer from post-traumatic stress disorder because they have had nothing to do since they fled from Myanmar. Now, they are suffering from some kind of mental imbalance. There are many NGOs here that deal with mental problems. Although mental health means mental wellbeing, Rohingya people think they are treating mad people. Therefore, they think that mentally sick people are being treated here. Why should we go to those who treat the mentally retarded? The family thinks that if they go to a mental hospital, they will be laughed at and talked about so much that they do not want to go there. (Interview: 2022MRN3)

However, women and young girls suffer more from different kinds of gender-specific problems and diseases. One such problem is the difficulty of maintaining personal hygiene. Women respondents explained how difficult it is to use public bathing and toilet facilities. One respondent told me,

NGOs have arranged toilets and showers for us, but they are far away from home, and many families share one or two toilets. As a result, girls cannot use the toilets during the day even if they want to. Because there are many boys and people on the way to the toilet, it is very difficult to go. Although the shower can be done at home, the toilet cannot be done anywhere else. As a result, we have to wait until the evening. In addition, if it is very important during the day, then we must wear a *burqa* to go to the toilet. It is very much a problem. (Interview: 2022MRF7)

Another respondent told me, 'Holding urination for a long time to find a suitable space to do it is creating infections among us, including myself' (Interview: 2022MRF8). Unfortunately, there do not seem to be any immediate solutions for toilets and water and bathing issues. One of the respondents told me they had requested the volunteers to increase the number of tube wells and toilets, but with no results yet. As she said, 'in our camp, we have only two toilets. We have requested our volunteers. Every time they come, they take the request list with them. However, we haven't seen any action yet' (Interview: 2022MRF8). In addition to urinary tract infections, all the respondents agreed that there is an increased prevalence of hepatitis A and B among males and females in the camps. However, an increase in infectious diseases has also led to divorce. As one of my respondents told me, 'As hepatitis increased in the camps, I have seen a woman who was infected with hepatitis B. Her husband didn't have the ability to treat her, and no NGOs helped her with the treatment. As a result, the man left his wife and got married to another woman. However, this woman's life is ruined, and she has four kids to take care of' (Interview: 2022MRF4). This relates to the issue of women's lack of agency, given that men have greater power to decide whom to live with.

There are several other gender-specific problems in the camps, including personal hygiene. For example, issues with menstrual hygiene are difficult to deal with, as it is attached to issues with Rohingya social structure, stigma, and the physical facilities in the camps. As one of my respondents explained,

NGOs provide girls with sanitary pads to use during periods. The sanitary pads provided cannot be dried inside the house or in the bathroom which are located outside of the house. However, when we were in Burma, we could let it dry nicely behind the bathroom, which no one could see but myself. Now if we let it dry in the bathroom, all sorts of people come in and see it! This is a shame. If you cannot let this thing dry in the sun, then the thing will not be usable, insects will come there. In addition, at home, it cannot be allowed to dry because the brothers are watching, and the father is watching. Because of this, the wet pad is being used repeatedly. Due to this, we are facing various diseases. (Interview: 2022MRF4)

ACCESS TO JUSTICE AND GENDER ISSUES IN THE CAMPS

During my interviews in the Rohingya camps, it became evident that the formal justice system in the camps is very limited, particularly as it relates to violence against women. As they have no access to the Bangladeshi formal legal system, women rely mainly on the informal justice mechanism. Some NGOs work on GBV and provide women a friendly space for counselling, or simply a place for women to meet and share experiences in the camps. Nevertheless, getting justice after domestic violence is quite difficult. One of the respondents, who is employed by an international organisation, shared with me that GBV survivors in the camps tend to avoid seeking refuge in the available safe shelters.[5] There are two primary reasons for this. First, there are numerous bureaucratic and administrative hurdles associated with accessing these shelters. For instance, an individual may urgently require shelter, but the CiC might need to contact relevant personnel, engage in discussions, and subsequently take some time to provide the necessary assistance. This prolonged process creates a sense of reluctance among survivors to utilise shelter facilities. Second, there is a social stigma surrounding these safe shelters. When survivors return to the community after their stay, they often encounter a cycle of violence and face numerous inquiries. The community members may question the survivor about her prolonged absence. A prevailing perception within the community is that women engage in transactional sex outside the camp during their absence. Consequently, the woman becomes stigmatised, leading to her reluctance to accept the offer of safe shelter. Furthermore, if the survivor has children, she faces additional challenges regarding their care. Questions arise regarding where she can leave her children and whether she can bring them along. If bringing the children is possible, the duration for which they can stay in the shelter becomes a concern. The safe shelter option thus becomes untenable for many survivors in such circumstances.

Often, violence against women, particularly sexual violence, goes unaddressed and remains silent because of the unavailability of services, existing social norms, and customary practices. Some *Majhi* might intervene in settling disputes (small-scale conflicts, family-related disputes, etc.) and the CiC becomes involved in it if the *Majhi* fails to settle the dispute. However, this process is quite complicated, as it is embedded in asymmetrical power relations and too bureaucratic. One of my respondents told me,

> In many cases, it is not possible to obtain proper justice from the *Majhi*. As the *Majhi* is always a man, and the perpetrator is also a man, he has more access to the *Majhi*. He can easily influence the *Majhi* to bring justice in his favour. I know perpetrators often bribe the *Majhi*. Therefore, women are always victims and do not get the justice they deserve. They receive unfair treatment from the *Majhi*. (Interview: 2023MRF1)

This informal justice system, as my respondent told me, often does not bring any punishment against the perpetrator. Rather, the offender is forced to ask for mercy from the victim and provide a written commitment that he will not repeat such an act of violence in the future. I asked this respondent why this is the standard. He replied that these days there is enormous insecurity and criminality in the camps. Moreover, the authorities aim to bring harmony and resolve disputes rather than punish the offenders. The government has recently withdrawn the military from the camps and deployed the Armed Police Battalion (APBn). During my last visit to the camps in 2023, it became clear that refugees want the military to be back in the camp for security and for resolving all other disputes in the camps. However, this is not likely to happen.

Another respondent told me why it is so difficult to reach the CiC. He said, 'We are a powerless human being living the camp. CiC sir is always surrounded by many people, such as his assistants and the *Majhi*. If you want to reach him for some reason, you must pass through so many people to reach him, and it can take even more than a year to reach him' (Interview:2023MRM2). Another respondent added, 'as it is a too lengthy and tiresome process which requires back-and-forth steps to reach CiC to get formal justice, women just abandon the hope for justice. In the end, women just accept injustice' (Interview: 2023 MRF1).

It was also reported[6] that after a six-year-old Rohingya girl was raped and found unconscious, the mother of the girl wanted to file a report with both Armed Police Battalion (APBn) and the CiC, but struggled. She recalled,

The APBn told me that, since it's a 'sensitive case,' I could only file a complaint with the CiC. I was determined to take legal action, but I need the support of the CiC or Bangladesh authorities to do so, since I'm Rohingya. It's not like I can just go to the police station like Bangladeshi people can. But unfortunately, the CiC didn't give me permission or even meet me again for another five days. (Human Rights Watch, 2023, para 52)

After her struggle, she managed to reach the local police, but the police denied her claim on the grounds of a false medical document. Now, she and her little daughter are in constant fear as they are threatened by the man who the girl identified as the rapist.

To date, all if the CiCs in Rohingya camps in Cox's Bazar have been male.[7] A female CiC, though a government official, might endeavour to acknowledge the plight of Rohingya females and intervene in GBV instances. While her capacity to ensure justice in such cases would be limited, she could play a significant role by recognising the vulnerabilities faced by Rohingya women and taking proactive steps to address and mitigate their challenges.

ARSA, GANGS, INSECURITY, AND WOMEN REFUGEES

It is clear from the different news media outlets that the camps are experiencing increased criminality, drug trafficking, and conflicts over the control of resources, particularly among young adults. One report claims that 'Arson, kidnapping, trafficking, drugs, and fights were listed as the most common crimes in the camps. 90% of those interviewed said that kidnappings were a problem' (Root, 2022, para 8). There is an enormous internal conflict among the contesting youth groups. As one of the respondents said, 'Before the murder of Mohibullah,[8] there was unity in the camps. If any problem and conflict were to happen in the camps, he would help to solve them. After his murder, the situation deteriorated in the camps. Nobody would listen to anybody. Everyone is against everyone' (Interview: 2022MRF5). Thus, it is important to understand how criminality and insecurity in camps affect women and young children. As women are facing multidimensional insecurities, many of the women respondents told me they became victims of public sexual harassment by Rohingya youths. As one of the respondents told me,

5 GENDERED VULNERABILITIES AND VIOLENCE IN ROHINGYA REFUGEE...   83

I feel scared to go out, particularly in the afternoon. Many times, when I went out during the afternoon, there were some young adults sitting idly on the street and doing nothing. They started following me and stalking me. I then started walking fast and stopped going where I intended to go. It has not happened just with me, also with many other young girls. (Interview: 2022MRF7)

Another form of insecurity stems from ARSA. News media in Bangladesh have reported that ARSA was involved in the killing of Rohingya leader Mohibullah, six murders in the camps, and extortion in the camps (Bdnews24.com, 2022). However, in an interview with a Bangladesh TV channel,[9] the chief of ARSA denied any connection to these killings (Jamuna Television, 2022). According to the police and news media, there are other 'terrorist' groups in the camps, such as 'Munna Bahini', fighting for control in the camps (Prothom Alo, 2022). According to a leading Bengali national newspaper, Daily Prothom Alo, 'Around 14 armed criminal gangs are active in the 34 Rohingya refugee camps in Ukhiya and Teknaf upazila in Cox's Bazar. Seven of these groups are active in Ukhiya and seven in Teknaf. These groups are involved in various crimes, including Yaba [a synthetic drug which combines methamphetamine and caffeine] and gold smuggling, kidnapping, extortion and human trafficking' (Prothom Alo, 2021, para 1). The presence of different terrorist groups in the camps poses security threats to the ordinary Rohingya and Bangladeshi states. When asked about what they know about ARSA, one respondent told me,

A bad group is born among the Rohingyas. Earlier, some Rohingyas left Pakistan, from which some people came back again. Then, some people came from Saudi Arabia. To be honest, the Rohingyas were not allowed to study, which is why they are still uneducated. Those uneducated people who came from outside, have formed a group within the Rohingya community. The main purpose of forming their party was to make the Arakan State independent. They demanded a contribution from the Rohingyas, saying that Arakan State would be independent. If anyone did not pay, he would be beaten up. In that way, there are many big and wise people among the Rohingyas; they used to ask them to go to Burma with them, and they also said that they will go to Burma to fight, they will need weapons, and for that, they need money. By saying this, they used to charge more money from them than usual and beat them if they did not pay. In addition, there is such a record that they killed many people before killing Master Mohibullah! (Interview: 2022MRM1)

It is also important to understand how this could threaten women's security in the camps. One respondent claimed that, although the extent of their presence in the camps varies, ARSA has committed extortion, forced marriage, and physical torture against some women. She stated that 'ARSA [members] forcibly marry women and often they marry multiple times' (Interview: 2022MRF9). Another respondent shared her story about how she was abducted and tortured by ARSA:

> I, along with another woman named Rokeya, were abducted by ARSA last year. As I was doing some community work, they abducted me and demanded money from me. However, I told them I don't have money. Then, my husband and other relatives negotiated with ARSA and released me after giving them a written commitment that I would not continue my work. However, I think it was not the main reason, since the wife of Munna who led a rival gang used to come to my community work, they abducted me to take revenge against the Munna gang. I was lucky that ARSA did not torture me. They kept Rokeya in custody for more than a week. Most often, when they abduct men, they torture a lot and often kill them. (Interview: 2023MRF1)

It is clear from the respondents that compared to men, women and young girls have strong feelings of insecurity, whether this comes from ARSA or any other gangs. As one respondent said, 'When talking about insecurity, the first thing that comes up is that we cannot move freely! We must always walk in fear! If we want to go outside, we feel that if the gangs want something from us and if we cannot give it, then they will torture us or even kidnap us. Therefore, we could not go out for these. When we had to go to the hospital or for various urgent needs, we were in fear of kidnapping. In addition, there are trafficking—people who sell women, we are more afraid of them!' (Interview: 2022MRM1).

Ordinary Rohingya, as they claimed during interviews, have no connection or interest in ARSA. One of the respondents told me, 'Since we came to Bangladesh from Myanmar, we have been seeing some miscreants using the name of ARSA doing some bad things' (Interview: 2022MRM3). Although only one of my respondents was kidnapped by ARSA, all the respondents claimed that they knew someone who was tortured by ARSA. Whether it is ARSA or other gangs in the camps, there is a clear increase in criminal activities in the camps. When asked why, my respondents identified many reasons, including the lack of job opportunities, no education, drug addiction, greed, engagement of a criminal gang from the host communities, the presence of Yaba smuggling routes in this area, the absence of military in the camps, the absence of the security police in the camps during the evening and at night, etc.

ROHINGYA MEN IN BANGLADESH: 'MONSTROUS OTHER' ON THE CREATION

It has been more than five years since the Rohingya were stranded in the camps in Bangladesh. Over the last few years, crimes, the drug trade, and murders have increased in the camps. According to the Daily Star, a leading national daily, Bangladesh Police databases show that at least 21 Rohingya individuals were murdered during a four-month period (June–October) in 2022. The police have filed approximately 2441 cases (1644 cases of drugs, 88 rape, 115 murder, and 39 abductions) against 5226 Rohingya over crimes at the Rohingya refugee camps (Khan & Yousuf, 2022). Although most local people in the host community were welcoming to the Rohingya, some of our respondents showed quite a negative attitude towards them, particularly those who became directly affected by their relocation. For example, during the first phase of interviews, one of my respondents, a small grocery shopkeeper near Camp Five, complained, 'Now I became a refugee myself'. When asked how that is possible, he replied,

> Look, I and my family have been living here in this place (next to the camp). You see, on the right side, I used to have my agricultural lands on which I used to live. However, now, you see, it's been taken by the government to rehabilitate the Rohingya. You see, part of the land of my house has been cut off, and the rest will go away soon. Don't I then become a refugee in my own land? (Interview: 2018LM5)

I observed the same kind of frustration among some of the respondents who were day labourers. During my interviews with them in Ukhiya, they told me how the Rohingya young men and children are taking their jobs away. One respondent told me, 'Rohingya children work almost for free in restaurants and in other shops now. It means less opportunity for us' (Interview: 2018LM4). However, on the contrary, a local shopkeeper in the same area told me, 'as the Rohingya came in an enormous number in the small place, it created a large demand on the local supply chain. Even small shops like one of mine are benefiting from this' (Interview: 2018LM6). Despite the initially welcoming attitude towards the Rohingya, people started becoming frustrated and felt deprived of international aid and other kinds of help. As time went on, the security situation worsened and criminal activities rose in the camps. This led to distrust, feelings of burden, and insecurity among the people in the host community. Local people started to think of Rohingya men as drug leaders and kidnappers and as a threat to the security of the region. To some, their 'Muslim brother' (Rohingya) has turned into a 'common enemy' (to the host). As one of the respondents told me, 'When they first arrived and asked for shelter in our land, knowing our Muslim brothers' sufferings in Myanmar, we became empathic toward them and welcomed them … It was such a mistake our people have done. These are criminals and Yaba traders. We now regret that we gave them shelter here' (Interview: 2023LM3). The host community has gradually become less and less sympathetic towards the Rohingya; as one of the respondents told me, 'Why should we care about these outsiders? They are job snatchers, resource destroyers and dakoits. They are becoming monsters' (Interview: 2023LM1). All the Rohingya respondents I interviewed during the second and third phases of my interviews agreed on the increased criminality in the camps. They listed the most common types of crime in the camps as harassment, extortion, kidnapping, illicit drug trade and consumption, and gang-based crime.

The feeling of insecurity among the host community also stems from thinking about the future of the Rohingya crisis. As one of the respondents told me, 'I don't think they will go back to Myanmar. I am worried about the future of our kids. When they mix up with them, their prospects will be ruined' (Interview: 2023LM3). In addition to these concerns, the presence of ARSA makes the camps and nearby areas more vulnerable to the rise of militancy, pushing the host community into further trouble.

Ordinary and Empowered Rohingya Women: Unpacking Complexities

During my interviews with local people in Cox's Bazar, one respondent told me, 'Rohingya women are looking for sympathy and attention from the presenting them as very vulnerable'. When asked why he thought so, he replied, 'they are probably lying about their sufferings to get attention. They are too conservative and lazy, doing nothing' (Interview: 2023LM3) Though this might not be a prevailing perception of the Rohingya women, a negative perception and an enemy discourse is under construction among the host community, as noted above. Yet, against all odds, some—if not many—Rohingya women are becoming empowered through different activities with gender-based programmes in the camps. Many Rohingya men and women have been working as volunteers in NGOs, including international and UN organisations. One respondent who works with such an organisation explained how she thinks the empowerment process is on its way to them. She explained, 'Now I work with CPJ [Centre for Peace and Justice, BRAC University] as a volunteer. I have been gaining work experience, and one day I hope I will achieve an even better position. My family gives importance to my opinion in decision making' (Interview: 2022MRF2). Like her, many men also work as volunteers and run their own refugee-led organisations (RLO). For example, one interviewee, who runs an RLO, believes that his organisation contributes to the empowerment of volunteers and other participants. A respondent named Nahar told me,

> When we came to Bangladesh, we learned about rights. Here, we learned that boys and girls have equal rights. I work with TDH [Terre des hommes] and UNHCR [United Nations High Commissioner for Refugees] from where I have learned many things. Having learned these things, I now feel much more aware. I am also trying to spread this knowledge among my Rohingya brothers and sisters. (Interview: 2022MRF5)

All the volunteers and leaders of the RLOs I interviewed are in a better position to claim their rights and are aware of their obligations to the community.

However, pathways to empowerment are not easy for these displaced people. Obstacles include the Rohingya social structure, gendered identity, (lack of) access to resources, and the camp governance structure. For example, one of my respondents told me,

> There are many of our Rohingyas who do not want girls to go out of the house. They think that girls are bad if they go out of the house. As a result, the girls who work and go out of the camp are looked down upon and considered bad girls. They think "why girls should work, there are boys for that". (Interview: 2022MRF7)

None of my male respondents, who also work as volunteers and run RLOs, faced the same problems as female respondents. Beyond this gendered social structural dimension, access to resources and human capital in the form of skills and education play a significant role. All the respondents who work as volunteers for different NGOs have a certain level of education and most of them are youth. Thus, relatively older and uneducated Rohingya are left out of such empowerment procedures. In addition, generally, no female works as a CiC in the camp. Understanding women's issues and providing support accordingly to the women remains a challenge due to the governance pattern of the camp. Moreover, there are restrictions on movement for the Rohingya, which makes it difficult for them to leave the camps. It eventually affects the empowerment procedures for the Rohingya.

CONCLUSION

The vulnerabilities of Rohingya men and women living in the refugee camps in Bangladesh are multidimensional and gendered. While they are still bearing mental trauma and physical scars, the securitisation of Rohingya refugees is in the making. Women are experiencing different structural, cultural, and symbolic violence in the forms of intimate partner violence, polygamy, child marriage, insecurity, and a lack of wellbeing. Many Rohingya men are becoming involved in crime. The host community's initial sympathy towards the Rohingya is turning into hostility and Muslim brotherhood to enmity. This form of 'othering' of the Rohingya community has led to the construction of the Rohingya men as a 'monstrous other'. It is, however, undeniable that in the camps, there is a different life—a highly unsecured and gang rule prevails. In the public psyche of the host community, the word 'Rohingya' is being used as an offensive term. Often, they use the term to tease someone or to indicate 'criminality'. Despite all odds, some of the Rohingya women are on the way to being empowered.

NOTES

1. See updated statistics on the Rohingya crisis in Bangladesh at the Refugee Relief and Repatriation Commissioner (RRRC) website at https://rrrc.gov. bd/. The childbirth data was obtained from: http://rrrc.gov.bd/site/ notices/b633c111-7526-4f01-84dc-6faef3a53463/-
2. The intricacies surrounding Prophet Muhammad's (Peace be upon Him) marital relationships, particularly his polygamous unions, necessitate

nuanced clarification. Notably, out of the 12 marriages attributed to him, it's discerned that only two were with women who were virgins, denoting a deeper motive beyond mere biological inclination. Noteworthy is the timeline of these unions: between the ages of 25 and 50, he was wedded to a sole spouse, while from 51 to 63, additional marriages were contracted for multifaceted purposes. These included extending protection and honour to widows to serve as exemplary models, emancipating slaves, fostering diplomatic ties for the propagation of Islam, personal affiliations with the Prophet, and challenging societal norms to impart profound moral lessons. To illuminate these facets further, readers are encouraged to explore 'The Concept of Polygamy and the Prophet's Marriages' authored by Sayyid Muhammed Rizvi (2006), see https://www.al-islam.org/articles/concept-polygamy-and-prophets-marriages-sayyid-muhammad-rizvi

3. As elaborated elsewhere in this book, marriage, polygamy, mixed marriages, and childbirth were subjected to control by the Myanmar military in the 1990s and again in 2015. However, radical Buddhist groups assert that Muslim Rohingya are depicted as polygamous and 'dangerously reproductive'. Despite a scarcity of data on marriage and fertility behavior before the military regime, some sources (e.g., Alam, 1999) claim that Rohingya practiced polygamy. Furthermore, interviews suggest that before the military regime, they were able to engage in polygamous unions, as permitted by Islamic traditions.

4. CiC is a government employee who has the overall responsibility for each designated camp. CiC oversees humanitarian actors, coordinates and liaises with government and security officials.

5. There are safe shelters inside the camps and in the nearby town called Cox's Bazar.

6. See the full report here: https://www.hrw.org/news/2023/07/13/bangladesh-spiraling-violence-against-rohingya-refugees

7. See the list of CiCs here: http://rrrc.portal.gov.bd/site/view/officer_list/%E0%A6%95%E0%A6%B0%E0%A7%8D%E0%A6%AE%E0%A6%95%E0%A6%B0%E0%A7%8D%E0%A6%A4%E0%A6%BE%E0%A6%AC%E0%A7%83%E0%A6%A8%E0%A7%8D%E0%A6%A6- (accessed June 10, 2023).

8. Mohibullah was the most prominent Rohingya leader, a peace activist and community organiser who co-founded Arakan Rohingya Society for Peace and Human Rights (ARSPH) in the Rohingya refugee camp in Bangladesh. He was assassinated on September 29, 2021. Bangladeshi Police he was murdered by the Arakan Rohingya Salvation Army (ARSA).

9. See interview of ARSA chief Ata Ullah with Jumana TV, February 24, 2022

REFERENCES

Agamben, G. (1998). *Homo Sacer: Sovereign Power and Bare Life* (D. Heller-Roazen, Trans.). Stanford University Press.

Alam, M. A. (1999). *A Historical Background of Arakan*. Chittagong, Bangladesh, Arakan Historical Society.

Bdnews24.com. (2022, June 13). Police Say ARSA Killed Rohingya Leader Mohib Ullah to Stop Refugee Repatriation. *Bdnews24.com*. https://bdnews24.com/bangladesh/police-say-arsa-killed-rohingya-leader-mohib-ullah-to-stop-refugee-repatriation, accessed on January 9, 2023.

Bourdieu, P. (1979). Symbolic Power. *Critique of Anthropology, 4*(13–14), 77–85. https://doi.org/10.1177/0308275x7900401307

Bourdieu, P., & Wacquant, L. (2004). Symbolic Violence. In N. Scheper-Hughes & P. Bourgois (Eds.), *Violence in War and Peace: An Anthology* (pp. 271–274). Wiley-Blackwell.

Galtung, J. (1996). Peace by Peaceful Means: Peace and Conflict. *Development and Civilization*. Sage. https://doi.org/10.4135/9781446221631

Human Rights Watch. (2023). *Bangladesh: Spiraling Violence Against Rohingya Refugees*. https://www.hrw.org/news/2023/07/13/bangladesh-spiraling-violence-against-rohingya-refugees, accessed on October 4, 2023.

International Rescue Committee. (2020). *The Shadow Pandemic: Gender-Based Violence among Rohingya refugees in Cox's Bazar*. https://www.rescue.org/sites/default/files/document/2247/theshadowpandemicbangladesh.pdf, accessed on September 25, 2021.

Jamuna Television. (2022). *ARSA Chief Ataullah*. https://www.youtube.com/watch?v=Vd2hWrNzxPk, accessed on September 30, 2022.

Khan, M. J., & Yousuf, M. (2022, October 28). Rohingya Refugee Camps: Killings on the Rise, Gangs on the Prowl. *The Daily Star*. https://www.thedailystar.net/news/bangladesh/crime-justice/news/rohingya-refugee-camps-killings-the-rise-gangs-the-prowl-3154056, accessed on January 8, 2023

Melnikas, A. J., Ainul, S., Ehsan, I., Haque, E., & Amin, S. (2020). Child Marriage Practices Among the Rohingya in Bangladesh. *Conflict and Health, 14*(1), 28. https://doi.org/10.1186/s13031-020-00274-0

Myanmar Ministry of Health and Sports (MoHS) and ICF. (2017). *Myanmar Demographic and Health Survey 2015–16*. Nay Pyi Taw, Myanmar, and Rockville, Maryland USA: Ministry of Health and Sports and ICF.

Oxfam International. (2018). *Rohingya Refugee Response Gender Analysis: Recognizing and Responding to Gender Inequalities*. O. International.

Prothom Alo. (2021, October 3). 14 Armed Groups Active in the Rohingya Camps. *Prothom Alo* https://en.prothomalo.com/bangladesh/crime-and-law/14-armed-groups-active-in-the-rohingya-camps, accessed on December 7, 2021.

Prothom Alo. (2022, June 23). Another ARSA Man Gunned Down in Cox's Bazar Rohingya Camp. *Prothom Alo*. https://en.prothomalo.com/bangladesh/local-news/another-arsa-man-gunned-down-in-coxs-bazar-rohingya-camp, accessed on January 22, 2023.

Radio Free Asia. (2022, April 13). Bangladesh Home Minister Claims Rohingya Have Babies to Get More Food Aid. *Radio Free Asia* https://www.rfa.org/english/news/myanmar/food-04132022170923.html, accessed on September 21, 2022.

Root, R. L. (2022, February 11). New Report Reveals 'Miserable' Conditions in Rohingya Refugee Camps. *devex*. https://www.devex.com/news/new-report-reveals-miserable-conditions-in-rohingya-refugee-camps-102616#:~:text=Arson%2C%20kidnapping%2C%20trafficking%2C%20drugs,put%20in%20prison%2C%20Ismail%20explained, accessed on September 28, 2022.

UNFPA. (2020). *Child Marriage in Humanitarian Settings in South Asia: Study Results from Bangladesh and Nepal*. U. R. UNFPA APRO. https://asiapacific.unfpa.org/en/publications/child-marriage-humanitarian-settings-south-asia

Whisnant, R. (2021). Feminist Perspectives on Rape. In E. N. Zalta (Ed.), *Stanford Encyclopedia of Philosophy*. Metaphysics Research Lab, Stanford University. https://plato.stanford.edu/entries/feminism-rape/, accessed on November 17, 2022.

Open Access This chapter is licensed under the terms of the Creative Commons Attribution 4.0 International License (http://creativecommons.org/licenses/by/4.0/), which permits use, sharing, adaptation, distribution and reproduction in any medium or format, as long as you give appropriate credit to the original author(s) and the source, provide a link to the Creative Commons license and indicate if changes were made.

The images or other third party material in this chapter are included in the chapter's Creative Commons license, unless indicated otherwise in a credit line to the material. If material is not included in the chapter's Creative Commons license and your intended use is not permitted by statutory regulation or exceeds the permitted use, you will need to obtain permission directly from the copyright holder.

CHAPTER 6

Conclusion

Abstract The Rohingya have experienced different forms of violence at different times and in different spaces. This chapter presents the summary of the book and explains the gender-differentiated forms of direct, structural, cultural, and symbolic violence experienced by the Rohingya in Myanmar and the camps in Bangladesh. At the end of this chapter, some recommendations are made to reduce gendered violence and vulnerabilities in the camps, such as introducing camp-based income-generating activities, strengthening refugee-led organisations, re-designing the *Majhi* system to include women, appointing women officials at the top level of refugee governance, and introducing 'mobile courts' in the camps to ensure gender justice.

Keywords Rohingya • Women • Gender justice • Violence

The forced migration of the Rohingya started in 1978. It worsened in 2012 and reached its climax in 2017. The atrocities committed by the Myanmar military and the denial of Myanmar citizenship have forced approximately one million Rohingya to seek refuge in neighbouring Bangladesh. While in Myanmar, the acts of murder, rape, and other forms of sexual violence carried out by the military have had devastating effects on the physical and psychological well-being of the refugees, continuing

© The Author(s) 2024
M. M. Salehin, *Gendered Vulnerabilities and Violence in Forced Migration*, https://doi.org/10.1007/978-3-031-62435-3_6

even after they arrived in Bangladesh. Many refugee women have never been able to fully recover from the traumatic experiences. Rather, they continue to experience different forms of violence in their country of destination, Bangladesh.

In a continuum of violence, the Rohingya experienced different forms of violence at different times and in different spaces. Following Galtung, I classified them as direct violence (murder, killings, physical injury and torture, rape, and other forms of sexual violence, perpetrated mainly by the Myanmar military), structural violence (pervasive poverty, discrimination in education and access to resources and services, patriarchy, and intimate partner violence) and cultural violence (religious and cultural logics that justify violence) (Galtung, 1969, 1990, 1996). In this book, I explored how these different forms of violence are gendered or how we could explain them from a gender perspective, using the lens of intersectionality.

As is evident from the existing news and research, violence erupted in 2012 with a gendered rumour about the rape of a Buddhist woman in Rakhine State by Muslim Rohingya men. Gendered narratives and rumours are recurrent in both everyday and elite discourses—particularly those that present Buddhist women as vulnerable to Muslim Rohingya violence, rape, and forced conversion to Islam—because they create a perceived need for the urgent protection of Buddhist women from Rohingya men. The military and ultra-nationalist Buddhists have systematically used religious and cultural reasonings to justify their actions and the violence against the Rohingya, depicting Rohingya men as an existential threat to Buddhism and the state. This is also reflected in the passing of four laws (i.e. Population Control Law, the Conversion Law, the Buddhist Women's Special Marriage Law, and the Monogamy Law) for the protection of race and religion (McCarthy & Menager, 2017). Rohingya men, therefore, have been portrayed as perpetrators of forced marriage and converting Buddhist women to Islam. They are 'violent extremists' and 'terrorists' practising 'violent Islam', wealthy and sexually deviant rapists. Thus, using a gendered linguistic narrative, Buddhist monks and the military emerged as protectors of their vulnerable women from the so-called Muslim rapist. Oppositely, Rohingya women have been portrayed as ugly and dangerously fertile breeders.

Long before this portrayal of the Rohingya, the term '*kala*' (or *Bengali Kala*), a derogatory term used to undermine the Rohingya as ignorant and lower-level human beings, was established. This mechanism of 'othering' became more prevalent during the post-2012 violence, as evidenced through hate speech, particularly on social media. Fear of the 'other' has turned the Rohingya into a 'radical other'. For Croft (2012, p. 87), 'radical others' is 'the most threatening form of other …, one that threatens the very existence of the self. Here, the Other becomes increasingly understood as a dehumanized monster as the sense of threat grows'. Distrust and violence against the Rohingya were also fuelled by inter-communal relations and enforced segregation. The 'threat image' of the Rohingya has a historical origin; animosity and distrust of the Rohingya can be connected to the anti-Indian riots in the 1930s and Japanese invasion in 1942. While some Rohingya acknowledged that the relationship between Muslims and Buddhists in Rakhine was more amicable before the conflicts of 2012, it significantly deteriorated in the aftermath of those events. The proliferation of hate speech, the increased use of derogatory and abusive language directed at the Rohingya, and the growing sense of insecurity further exacerbated the situation for the Rohingya community.

In order to comprehend the violence against the Rohingya population, it is imperative to consider the structural, cultural, and symbolic forms of violence, as well as their gendered nature. Structurally, the denial of education, limited mobility, and pervasive poverty in Rakhine State are embedded in Myanmar's governance policy. As agreed by the respondents, the opportunity for higher education above primary, and in some cases secondary, level was limited, more so if they were women. Many of these crises are rooted in the 'development crisis' in Rakhine State. A report from the Advisory Commission on Rakhine State states that the poverty rate in the state (Rakhine) stands at 78 percent, nearly twice the national average of 37.54 percent (Advisory commission on Rakhine State, 2017). This places it among the most economically disadvantaged regions in the country. In Rakhine State, all communities face economic hardship, a lack of adequate social services, and limited livelihood opportunities. Yet, women are more vulnerable than men in almost all aspects of life and livelihood, including uneven pay at work, lack of or difficult access to institutional loans (particularly for the unmarried and widows), and lack of rights to inheritance. Although the out-migration of women is higher in Rakhine, the migration of men poses an extra burden and workload on those women left behind in the community. Women's political and civic participation in Rakhine is almost absent. Muslim women in Rakhine State have had a lower level of education and movement restrictions, which has led to fewer life choices for them (Advisory Commission on Rakhine State, 2017). This limitation of movement, particularly for Muslims, is also connected to the Muslim religious practices and patriarchal structure of the community. Imposing movement restrictions leads to the inability to attend education and other social services by the Rohingya. Ultimately, this has created an inability of the Rohingya to participate in civic and political life.

The violence perpetrated against the Rohingya by the military is distinctly gendered, involving both sexual and non-sexual acts of violence. For instance, the targeting of young girls for molestation by the military and security forces on their way to and from home was intended to instil fear and anxiety, instigate shame (*beizzot gorá*), and limit mobility for the female members of the Rohingya community. Rape as a form of sexual violence and the forced witnessing of rape have been used as a mechanism for ethnic cleansing; the acts served to perpetuate the social stigma associated with such acts, humiliate one's dignity, intensify fear, and ultimately compel the Rohingya to flee their home country. Also, rape and other forms of sexual violence were directly chosen to undermine Rohingya women's reproductive capacity and motherhood. Additional acts of violence, such as the forced witnessing of rape by members of the family, gang rape, and sexual violence against men, represent a tendency toward 'militarised hypermasculinity' among the perpetrators, i.e. Myanmar military. Moreover, sexual violence against the Rohingya was systematic and 'itself an authorized policy, not a tolerated practice' by the Myanmar military (Alam & Wood, 2022, p. 10). What is intriguing here are the links between the nationalist Buddhists, the state, and the military and their use of racialised and gendered discourses to legitimise violence against the Muslim Rohingya minority in Myanmar. This has serious implications for further marginalisation and violence against the Muslim minority. As this book has shown, the perpetrators used hate speech, fake news, and disinformation—through the use of popular social media outlets, such as Facebook, and other technological devices, such as CDs and DVDs—to securitise the Muslim Rohingya and legitimise violence against them. In everyday discourse and practices, including schools and social spaces, the use of *Bengali Kala* has become a prevalent symbol of producing boundaries between the Rohingya and the Burmese.

Nevertheless, the arrival of this precarious population to Bangladesh did not end their sufferings. Many of them expressed their frustration and anger over not being able to return to their motherland, as well as dissatisfaction over the living conditions in the camps. Insecurity, whether it comes from a lack of physical safety or from economic and social crises, has become part of everyday life for the Rohingya living in the camps. Refugee camps have become a regular source of drug dealing, crime, murders, and gang violence, creating a sense of terror and insecurity among the camp residents. On the other hand, the rising criminality in and around the camps, resource scarcity, and economic and social stress have led to growing dissatisfaction among the host community. This has resulted in increased anti-Rohingya sentiments among the host community, both at the level of the discourse and practice. Here, construction of the Rohingya as a 'Monstrous Other' is underway, which is the same as a 'Radical Other' (Croft, 2012). During my interviews with the locals in Ukhia and Cox's Bazar, resentment was already widespread among Bangladeshis living near the camps. Some of these expressions were: 'We cannot bear the burden of them anymore', 'They must go back home', 'They are destroying our environment', 'Why should care about them, they are not one of us', 'They are threatening our tourism industry', 'They took our jobs', 'They must go back to Myanmar', 'They are criminals', etc. Bangladeshi media has presented the criminality, gang violence, and threats of violence from ARSA (Arakan Rohingya Salvation Army) and RSO (Rohingya Solidarity Organisation) as a threat to secular politics in Bangladesh in order to dehumanise the Rohingya. The initially positive narrative about the Rohingya soon shifted towards a negative one. As Crisp et al. (2023, p. para 3) claim,

> the media focused on the economic strain the refugees placed on the host country. Reports of environmental destruction and rapid population growth among the refugees became widespread. Politicians labelled the Rohingya as a 'security risk', resulting in harsh policies such as internet restrictions, SIM card confiscations, barbed wire fencing, forced repatriation, and relocating refugees to the isolated Bhashan Char. Local media in Ukhiya and Teknaf have played a significant role in fuelling anti-Rohingya sentiments, presenting a one-dimensional image of the Rohingya as a threat and a burden. These media outlets have skillfully exploited Facebook's algorithms to amplify their negative narratives, further contributing to the marginalisation of the Rohingya community.

The growing sense of insecurity among the host communities regarding the Rohingya in general, and men in particular, is also gendered. Rohingya men are often represented as a source of criminality and a threat to the security of the local host communities. On the contrary, Rohingya women are considered vulnerable and in need of help and protection. They also have been considered as more religious, which justifies mixed marriages between the Rohingya women and Bangladeshi men.

In the camps, a prevalent form of structural violence is the imposition of movement restrictions and the severe lack of viable livelihood opportunities. Consequently, this situation leads to a sense of powerlessness and discontent among Rohingya men, as they face considerable challenges in sustaining a means of living for their families. Like all patriarchal societies, the patriarchal structure of Rohingya society places men at the centre of protecting and maintaining the family. Failing to uphold such an obligation is equivalent to meaninglessness and powerlessness among the Rohingya. The resulting idleness among some men drives them to illicit activities, stemming from their hopelessness and disempowerment. This distress and a sense of powerlessness frequently culminate in instances of violence against their partners. Furthermore, this condition has encouraged some Rohingya men to engage in multiple marriages, seen as a form of 'business' and a potential income source within their community. Many young Rohingya girls have become victims of stalking and harassment by many such idle Rohingya youths in the camps. This, as a result, has produced insecurities among the Rohingya women and the imposition of restrictions on their movement, particularly during the night.

As highlighted by many of the individuals interviewed, the absence of livelihood opportunities within the camp and the lack of prospects for the repatriation of Rohingya to Myanmar have led many men to consider perilous sea journeys in a quest to reach other countries, such as India and Indonesia. Conversely, the circumstances for girls and women within the camps are even more precarious. Often men are more exposed to movement restrictions, leading to female Rohingya to search for jobs and go out of the camps. In many incidences, women were not searched on their way to work by security personnel at different checkpoints adjacent to the camps. However, this has also led women to a dialectical condition, as many women do not want to leave their houses due to the issue of seclusion (maintaining *forda*) and Islamic piety, but on the other hand, they have been forced to leave in search of a livelihood.

The financial hardship and lack of living space, as my respondents claim, has led to the prevalence of child marriages among the Rohingya. However, other structural issues such as traditional and Muslim gender norms, lack of education, and the accompanying social stigma associated with old-maidhood has led to child marriage and justification for the practice. Many Rohingya also think setting marriage early for their girls is a way to provide a shield against insecurity (physical, financial, and social) for the young girls. One of the consequences has been Rohingya women and girls becoming victims of violence, including intimate partner violence. However, both child marriage and intimate partner violence have been considered by many Rohingya women as the 'natural order' (symbolic violence). Intimate partner violence has been justified as the right of the man, who is responsible for the life and living of his women. As ARSA is active in the camps, both ordinary men and women have become victims of violence committed by ARSA. Yet, ARSA members forcibly marrying women in the camp has posed an extra burden and a source of violence against women.

The same woman who became a victim of direct violence in Myanmar continues to become a victim of structural violence in Bangladesh through patriarchal practices and a lack of access to justice. Those women and girls who fall victim to violence often struggle to obtain justice, due to the absence of a formal justice system within the camps, challenges in accessing the camp administration, and instances of corruption among some *Majhis* who serve as contact points for camp issues. As patriarchal and masculine protectionism prevails in the Rohingya social structure and is practiced in the camps, it is difficult for female victims of domestic violence to get justice. I concur with one of my respondents who expressed, 'They [*Majhi*] are men and men will favour men [perpetrators of violence]'. Thus, many women do not expect justice and instead have adjusted to living and coping with ongoing violence. Also, prevailing gender norms and social stigma—for example, the practice of women maintain seclusion (*forda*) and avoiding public spaces—has also made women reluctant to receive services (i.e., safe space) offered by NGOs for the victims of domestic and intimate partner violence.

Another source of vulnerability, especially for women, is associated with health and personal hygiene. Gender-insensitive camp structures and services make it nearly impossible for them to use public toilets and bathing facilities during the day. Many women tend to hold their bladders for a long time, leading to health issues. The situation worsens when it comes to menstrual hygiene, due to lack of access to hygiene products, stigmas around menstruation (i.e., drying undergarments and hygiene kits in public), and congested living conditions. Infectious diseases, such as hepatitis A & B, have had significant impacts on women's lives, including instances of divorce and abandonment by husbands. This attests to the lack of agency and power of Rohingya women vis-à-vis men. This also illustrates men's dualistic character, as they prioritise Islamic piety (for multiple marriage) on the one hand, while on the other, they disregard the same when they divorce or abandon their sick wives.

Efforts to resolve the Rohingya crisis have been mostly unsuccessful, leaving few prospects six years after the Rohingyas' forced migration to Bangladesh. They are still living in painstaking conditions in refugee camps. However, Rohingya youth, both male and female, have been participating in many different social and income-generating activities. For example, many young Rohingya women work as paid volunteers for national and international organisations working within the camps. Many of these women feel more empowered than they might have in Myanmar. Moreover, many Rohingya youth are very active on social media and organise different activities, including educating Rohingya children, transporting patients, organising cultural events, and making the everyday struggles of the Rohingya visible through different art media in the camps. Many of these youth also formed voluntary organisations in the camps, which I termed Refugee-led Organisations (RLOs). These RLOs, though predominantly led by the male Rohingya, have made some very important contributions to the community. Initiatives need to be taken by the authorities to strengthen these organisations based in the camps. Bangladeshi authorities, with help from international donors and camp-based organisations, should seriously explore the possibility of introducing economic and livelihood activities within the Rohingya refugee camps in Cox's Bazar. Allowing the Rohingya to participate in income-generating activities without leaving the camp 'will likely have many positive effects, and the positive aspects are anticipated to outweigh the negative ones' (Salehin & Rahman, 2023, para 19).

In Bangladesh, strong partnerships between government, NGOs, RLOs and other stakeholders in the camps are necessary for ending gender-based violence and vulnerabilities. It is also important to invest more in re-designing gender-sensitive infrastructure (both physical and social) and programmes in the camps. Separate toilet and shower facilities for women only are urgently needed. The women-centric 'Safe Space' programme, which offers women a space to meet and learn about their rights, needs to be re-evaluated to make it more user friendly and to minimise the stigma associated with its use. Gender justice in the camp needs special attention. To provide gender justice, introducing a 'mobile court' in the camp to ensure women can access justice and appointing women government officials at the top camp management level (e.g., CiC) might help. For better camp governance, the *Majhi* system, which is exclusively male dominated, needs to be redesigned to ensure accountability, to reduce abuses of power, and to include women as *Head Majhi and Majhi*.

REFERENCES

Advisory commission on Rakhine State. (2017). *Towards a Peaceful, Fair and Prosperous Future for the People of Rakhine*. State Counsellor of the Republic of the Union of Myanmar and in collaboration with the Kofi Annan Foundation. chrome-extension://efaidnbmnnnibpcajpcglclefindmkaj/https://www.kofiannanfoundation.org/app/uploads/2017/08/FinalReport_Eng.pdf, accessed on April 23, 2020.

Alam, M., & Wood, E. J. (2022). Ideology and the Implicit Authorization of Violence as Policy: The Myanmar Military's Conflict-Related Sexual Violence against the Rohingya. *Journal of global security studies, 7*(2). https://doi.org/10.1093/jogss/ogac010

Crisp, J., Rahman, S., Gunness, C., Lenin, R. R., & Zarni, M. (2023, May 3). How the Media Helped Shape a Negative Perception of the Rohingya. *The Daily Star.* https://www.thedailystar.net/opinion/views/news/how-the-media-helped-shape-negative-perception-the-rohingya-3310146, accessed on May 5, 2023.

Croft, S. (2012). Securitizing Islam: Identity and the Search for Security. *Cambridge University Press.* https://doi.org/10.1017/CBO9781139104142

Galtung, J. (1969). Violence, Peace, and Peace Research. *Journal of Peace Research, 6*(3), 167–191. http://www.jstor.org/stable/422690

Galtung, J. (1990). Cultural Violence. *Journal of Peace Research, 27*(3), 291–305. https://doi.org/10.1177/0022343390027003005.

Galtung, J. (1996). *Peace by Peaceful Means: Peace and Conflict, Development and Civilization*. Sage. https://doi.org/10.4135/9781446221631

McCarthy, G., & Menager, J. (2017). Gendered Rumours and the Muslim Scapegoat in Myanmar's Transition. *Journal of Contemporary Asia, 47*(3), 396–412. https://doi.org/10.1080/00472336.2017.1304563

Salehin, M. M., & Rahman, M. (2023, April 12). Unlocking Opportunities: Income Generation for Rohingya Refugees in Bangladesh. *PRIO Blogs.*

https://blogs.prio.org/2023/11/unlocking-opportunities-income-generation-for-rohingya-refugees-in-bangladesh/?fbclid=IwZXh0bgNhZW0C MTEAAR2dbdZaXfgJYSp17WxzzaHQygf0QtWi3JogFzkktsHTwp G5ivqTzeC5Zbw_aem_AckcwbK94HZhUlZJgUat27EW_K0BRbtORTA mtgizvIvAv7alyY5I2si4cqEKAbL0oi7J4ZeQPfLuyRkDFglI_2kb, accessed on April 12, 2024.

Open Access This chapter is licensed under the terms of the Creative Commons Attribution 4.0 International License (http://creativecommons.org/licenses/by/4.0/), which permits use, sharing, adaptation, distribution and reproduction in any medium or format, as long as you give appropriate credit to the original author(s) and the source, provide a link to the Creative Commons license and indicate if changes were made.

The images or other third party material in this chapter are included in the chapter's Creative Commons license, unless indicated otherwise in a credit line to the material. If material is not included in the chapter's Creative Commons license and your intended use is not permitted by statutory regulation or exceeds the permitted use, you will need to obtain permission directly from the copyright holder.

Index[1]

A

Abortion, 70, 71
Abuses of power, 101
Access to resources, 14, 17, 22, 38, 70, 72, 74, 87, 88, 94
Accountability, 59, 101
Age, 14, 20, 21, 32, 70, 73, 75, 77, 89n2
Agency, 62, 73, 74, 79, 100
Allah, 33, 34, 58, 73
Amnesty International, 35, 36
Anal rape, 57
Anti-Muslim, 32, 34, 37, 47
Arakan, 28, 29, 35, 49, 83
Arakan Rohingya Salvation Army (ARSA), 6, 31–36, 38, 82–86, 89n8, 97, 99
Armed Police Battalion (APBn), 81–82
Asylum seekers, 13, 14

B

Bangladesh, 2–6, 7n5, 13, 19, 21, 22, 27–30, 32, 34, 36, 38, 39n6, 39n7, 46, 48, 51, 53, 54, 59, 60, 64, 69–88, 89n8, 93, 94, 97, 99, 100
Bare life, 70
Bengali, 28, 29, 38, 39n7, 46, 47, 49–51, 54, 55, 83, 94, 96
Birth control, 59, 73, 74
Bismillah ar-Rahman ar-Rahim, 33
Bourdieu, P., 2, 4, 6, 12, 16–19, 21, 72, 74
Boycott, 30, 48
Buddha, 33, 36, 37
Buddha Dhamma Parahita Foundation, 32, 34
Buddhism, 3, 6, 29, 33–35, 37, 46–50, 54, 60, 61, 63, 94
Buddhist, 2, 3, 6, 18, 28, 30–38, 46–49, 51–55, 60–64, 75, 89n3, 94–96

---

[1] Note: Page numbers followed by 'n' refer to notes.

© The Author(s) 2024
M. M. Salehin, *Gendered Vulnerabilities and Violence in Forced Migration*, https://doi.org/10.1007/978-3-031-62435-3

103

104 INDEX

Burma, 3, 28, 29, 33, 35, 50, 51,
    62, 79, 83
Burmeseness, 46
Burning, 38, 47, 57, 62
Burqa, 58, 64n3, 79

C
Camp-in-Charge (CiC), 71, 78,
    80–82, 88, 89n4, 101
Castration, 57
Centre for Peace and Justice, BRAC
    University (CPJ), 5, 87
Checkpoint, 98
Child marriage, 6, 73–78, 88, 99
Christianity, 50
Citizenship, 28, 29, 35, 38, 57, 93
Citizenship Law of 1982, 29
Class, 18, 20, 21, 50, 51, 54, 74
Cockburn, C., 4, 12, 19, 21
Collective ownership, 49
Common enemy, 29, 38, 86
Constitution of the Union of
    Burma, 28
Continuum of violence, 4, 12,
    19–21, 94
Contraception, 58–59
Control, 57, 59, 72–75, 82, 83, 89n3
Cox's Bazar, 4–6, 7n5, 14, 32, 64, 69,
    73, 76, 82, 83, 86, 89n5, 97, 100
Crenshaw, K., 12, 20
Crime, 33, 82, 83, 85, 86, 88, 97
Cultural violence, 7n1, 12, 15–19, 21,
    30, 51, 74, 94

D
Daw Aung San Suu Kyi, 31, 47
Decision making, 59, 87
Dhamma School, 61, 62
Dhamma Wunthanu Rakhita, 32
Dignity, 96

Discrimination, 6, 12, 14, 15, 38,
    58–59, 63, 72, 94
Disempowerment, 98
Displacement, 1, 5, 6, 11, 12, 15, 21,
    27, 30, 38, 55, 58, 64, 69
Domestic violence, 6, 13,
    70–73, 80, 99
Domination, 2, 16–20
Dowry, 72, 75
Drug, 82, 83, 85, 86, 97

E
Early marriage, 72, 76, 77
Economic and social stress, 97
Education, 50, 58, 61, 63, 70, 72–74,
    76, 85, 88, 94–96, 99
Emotional abuse, 14
Empowerment, 87, 88
Environment, 97
Essentialism, 20
Ethnic cleansing, 57, 96
Ethnography, 4
Everyday racism, 49–51
Existential threat, 6, 34, 46–49, 94

F
Facebook, 37, 46–48, 63, 96, 97
Faith-based organisations, 61
Fake news, 32, 35, 52, 96
Far right, 32, 33
Fear, 32, 34, 47, 59, 70, 77, 82,
    84, 95, 96
Fertility, 73–78, 89n3
Financial, 70, 75, 99
Food aid, 58, 73
Forced conversion, 46, 48, 52, 62, 94
Forced migration, 1–6, 11–22,
    29, 93, 100
Forced relocation, 30, 78
Forced witness of rape, 56, 57, 96

INDEX

G

Galtung, J., 2, 4, 6, 7n1, 12, 13, 15–19, 21, 22n1, 71, 94
Gangs, 30, 31, 82–85, 88, 96, 97
Gender, 2–6, 11–22, 49, 51, 52, 58, 70–72, 78, 80–82, 94, 99, 101
Gendered, 2–6, 12–15, 17, 19–22, 32–34, 38, 45–64, 69–88, 94–96, 98
Gender-insensitive, 99
Governance, 36, 39n6, 87, 88, 95, 101

H

Halal, 34
Harakah Al Yaqeen, 31
Hepatitis A, 79, 100
Hepatitis B, 79, 100
Hindu, 7n2, 31–33, 35, 36, 50
Hinduism, 50
Humiliation, 57, 72
Hygiene, 6, 78–80, 99, 100
Hyper-fertile, 54

I

Income-generating activities, 100
Indian, 28, 49, 50
Indophobia, 50
Infrastructure, 100
Insecurity, 6, 20, 58, 76, 81–84, 86, 88, 95, 97–99
Insults, 15, 72
Intermarriage, 6, 46, 60–61
International Criminal Court (ICC), 36
International Crisis Group (ICG), 30, 61, 62
Intersectionality, 12, 19–21, 94
Intimate partner violence (IPV), 2, 12–14, 59, 88, 94, 99
Islamophobia, 17, 50

J

Justice, 6, 17, 22, 58–59, 80–82, 99, 101

K

Kala, 46, 49–51, 94, 96
Killing, 2, 3, 17, 22n1, 30, 36, 38, 53, 83, 94

L

Legitimate, 16, 17, 52
LGBTQ, 13, 15
Livelihood, 2, 55, 72, 75, 95, 98, 100

M

Ma Ba Tha (Organization for the Protection of Race and Religion), 2–3, 32–34, 37, 47, 55, 60–62
Magh, 35, 39n7, 49, 53, 59, 60, 62, 63
Majhi/Majhi, 5, 35, 39n6, 59, 71, 81, 99, 101
Male-dominated/Male dominated, 62, 101
Male survivors, 56
Marriage, 2, 6, 14, 17, 19, 46, 52, 59–62, 64, 72–78, 84, 88, 89n2, 89n3, 94, 98–100
Matrix of social forces, 20
Menstruation, 76, 100
Mental trauma, 70, 78–80, 88
Migration, 1–6, 11–22, 29, 93, 95, 100
Militarised hypermasculinity, 96
Military, 2, 6, 18, 22, 28–32, 35–38, 46, 47, 49–59, 61–64, 70, 73–76, 81, 85, 89n3, 93, 94, 96
Minority, 2, 8n7, 12, 14, 20, 32, 33, 37, 58, 61, 63, 96
Mis/disinformation, 46, 52, 96
Mixed marriages, 52, 89n3, 98

106 INDEX

Mobile court, 101
Mobility, 6, 38, 58–59, 95, 96
Mohibullah, 82, 83, 89n8
Monk, 28–31, 33, 34, 36–38, 46, 47,
  49, 50, 52, 54, 55, 60–61, 63, 94
Monstrous Other, 6, 46–49,
  85–86, 88, 97
Motherhood, 6, 46, 55, 63, 64, 96
Mrauk U, 30
Multiple marriage, 2, 6, 17,
  72–78, 98, 100
Munna Bahini, 83
Murder, 3, 16, 17, 37, 38, 52, 63, 82,
  83, 85, 93, 94, 97
Muslim, 2, 3, 7n2, 28–35, 37,
  46–52, 54, 55, 58, 60–63,
  64n3, 75, 86, 88, 89n3,
  94–96, 99
Mutilation, 57
Myanmar, 2–4, 6, 7n2, 7n3,
  18, 19, 21, 22, 27–38,
  39n7, 45–64, 69, 70, 72,
  74, 75, 78, 84, 86,
  89n3, 93–100
Myo-chit, 32

N
Nasaka, 31
National Democratic Party for
  Development (NDPD), 32
Negative coping, 75, 77
Ne Win, 37
NGOs, 71, 73, 78–80, 87,
  88, 99, 100
969, 2, 3, 32–34, 37
Northern Rakhine, 30, 58

O
Operation Dragon King, 29
Ordinary, 3, 30, 35, 38, 63, 78, 83,
  84, 86–88, 99
Othering, 88, 95

P
Patriarchy, 1, 17, 62, 74, 94
Penis amputation, 57
Performative rape, 56–58
Personal hygiene, 6, 78–80, 99
Physical, 1, 12–17, 19, 55, 57, 62, 63,
  70, 71, 76, 79, 84, 88, 93, 94,
  97, 99, 100
Poisonous snake, 52
Population Control Law, 61, 94
Posttruth politics, 32
Poverty, 2, 38, 63, 76, 94, 95
Power, 16–21, 29, 54, 59, 70, 79, 81,
  100, 101
Powerlessness, 98
Precarious conditions, 70
Pregnant, 70, 71
Propaganda, 34, 37, 47, 49, 52
Prophet Muhammad, 74, 89n2
Protector, 49, 51, 52, 55, 56, 94
Psychological abuse, 14, 72
Psychological harm, 1, 16, 72
Psychological stress, 69
Psychological trauma, 2, 6

Q
Quasidemocracy, 36

R
Race, 3, 20, 21, 28, 29, 39n3, 48,
  52, 60, 94
Radical other/Radical Other, 95, 97
Rakhine, 2, 4, 7n3, 30, 31, 35, 49, 50,
  53, 75, 95, 96
Rakhine Nationalities Development
  Party (RNDP), 32
Rakhine State, 2–4, 6, 7n3, 28–32, 35,
  37, 46, 49, 51, 58, 59, 63, 70,
  73, 74, 76, 94–96
Rape, 2, 3, 14, 17, 27, 30, 38, 48,
  51–58, 62, 63, 70, 71, 85,
  93, 94, 96

INDEX   107

Rapist, 30, 51, 52, 82, 94
Refugee, 3, 5, 6, 7n5, 12–15, 19–20,
    22, 29, 39n6, 46, 53, 55, 57–59,
    69–88, 93, 94, 97, 100
Refugee camp, 4, 6, 54, 58, 64,
    69–88, 89n8, 97, 100
Refugee-led organisations/Refugee-
    Led Organisations (RLOs), 5,
    59, 87, 100
Relief, 61, 77
Religion, 2, 3, 16, 20, 21, 32, 33, 36,
    37, 48, 60–62, 64, 73, 74, 77, 94
Repatriation, 13, 97, 98
Reproduction, 6, 19, 46, 52,
    55, 57, 63
Restricted mobility, 38, 58
Riots, 30, 31, 34, 47, 51, 95
Rohang, 28
Rohingya, 2–7, 7n2, 7n4, 7n5, 8n7,
    12–15, 17–21, 27–38, 39n6,
    45–64, 69–88, 89n3,
    89n8, 93–100
Rohingya girls, 53, 64, 81, 98
Rohingya Solidarity Organisation
    (RSO), 97
Rumour, 6, 27, 46, 49, 51–53, 94
Rwandan genocide, 51

S
Safe space/Safe Space, 99, 101
Safety, 5, 61, 97
Saffron Revolution/Saffron
    revolution, 36–38
Saudi Arabia, 35, 83
Scapegoat, 29
Sea journeys, 98
Security, 2, 13, 30, 31, 35, 38, 52, 81,
    83–86, 89n4, 96–98
Security force, 30–32, 38, 81, 96
Sermon, 46–48
786, 33

Sex, 19, 52, 56, 80
Sexual abuse, 57
Sexual and gender-based violence
    (SGBV), 2, 12, 14–15, 19,
    21, 54, 59
Sexual assault, 2, 14, 59
Sexual violence, 1–3, 6, 11–14, 22,
    38, 46, 52–59, 63–64, 70–72, 76,
    80, 93, 94, 96
Shame, 54, 56, 57, 70, 73, 80, 96
Social fabric, 57
Social media, 30, 34, 37, 46, 47, 49,
    51, 52, 63, 95, 96, 100
South Asia, 33
State Law and Order Restoration
    Council (SLORC), 29, 30
State Sangha Maha Nayaka
    Committee, 34
Stigma, 2, 22, 56, 64, 70, 73, 79, 80,
    96, 99–101
Structural violence, 16–21, 38,
    49, 58, 63, 71, 73,
    94, 98, 99
Symbolic violence, 4, 12, 15–19,
    21–22, 64, 70, 72, 74, 88, 99
Systems of domination, 17

T
Taing-yin-tha, 28
Tatmadaw, 31, 59
Teasing, 77
Teknaf, 7n5, 83, 97
Terror, 37, 47, 57, 64n2, 97
Terrorists, 47, 83, 94
Than Shwe, 37
Thien Sien, 37
Tourism, 97
Traditional gender norms, 17, 71
Traditional structure, 70
Trafficking, 2, 12, 14, 82–84
Transgender, 8n7

U

Ugly, 52, 55, 94
Ukhia, 5, 7n5, 97
Ukhiya, 83, 85, 97
Ultra-nationalism, 6
Ultranationalist, 28, 32–38, 47, 49, 54, 60–62
Unequal power, 16, 17
United Nations (UN), 2, 14, 28, 55, 87
United Nations High Commissioner for Refugees (UNHCR), 1, 3, 14, 30, 87
Unmarried, 70, 76, 77, 95
Urinary tract infections, 79

V

Victim, 2, 15, 17, 22, 38, 51, 53, 54, 56, 57, 59, 64, 71, 81, 82, 98, 99

Violence, 1–6, 7n1, 11–22, 22n1, 27, 28, 30–35, 37–38, 45–64, 69–88, 93–100
Violent Islam, 47, 94
Vulnerabilities, 2–7, 11–22, 38, 45–64, 69–88, 99, 100

W

Wellbeing/Well-being, 55, 71, 78, 88
Western biases, 20
Wirathu, Ashin, 33, 34, 36, 37, 47–49, 64n2

Y

Yaba, 83, 85, 86
Yangoon, 31
Youths, 15, 32, 35, 61, 82, 88, 98, 100